Books of Merit

BRIAN FAWCETT

HUMAN
happiness

THOMAS ALLEN PUBLISHERS

TORONTO

Library and Archives Canada Cataloguing in Publication

Fawcett, Brian, 1944–
Human happiness / Brian Fawcett.

ISBN 978-0-88762-808-5

1. Fawcett, Brian, 1944-. 2. Fawcett, Brian, 1944-   —Family.
3. Authors, Canadian (English)—20th century—Biography. I. Title.

PS8561.A94Z468 2011   c813'.54   C2011-903593-6

Editor: Patrick Crean
Cover design: Sputnik Design
Cover image: courtesy of the author
Text design: Gordon Robertson

Published by Thomas Allen Publishers,
a division of Thomas Allen & Son Limited,
390 Steelcase Road East,
Markham, Ontario L3R 1G2 Canada

www.thomasallen.ca

ONTARIO ARTS COUNCIL
CONSEIL DES ARTS DE L'ONTARIO

Canada Council
for the Arts

The publisher gratefully acknowledges the support of
the Ontario Arts Council for its publishing program.

We acknowledge the support of the Canada Council for the Arts, which
last year invested $20.1 million in writing and publishing throughout Canada.

We acknowledge the Government of Ontario through the
Ontario Media Development Corporation's Ontario Book Initiative.

We acknowledge the financial support of the Government of Canada
through the Canada Book Fund for our publishing activities.

11 12 13 14 15   5 4 3 2 1

Text printed on a 30% PCW recycled content and FSC certified stock

Printed and bound in Canada

*H*APPINESS is most often defined as a state of mind similar to, but more encompassing than, contentment, satisfaction, pleasure, or joy: what you are to yourself rather than what you feel at any given moment or are seen to be by others.

In the distant past happiness was associated with the Greek word *"Eudamonia"*: living a good life, which is to say, without being under threat from barbarians (however one defines them) or the gods.

Happiness is central to Buddhist thinking, which focuses on gaining freedom from suffering by following an Eightfold Path aimed ultimately at overcoming desire. In the last half of the twentieth century both happiness and desire became more closely linked with shopping, and in the twenty-first it has become a consumer commodity in and of itself, usually linked to disposable income and Oprah Winfrey–level therapy or, in some cultures, with detonating bandoliers of C5 explosives amongst the infidels so you can go to a heaven filled with voluptuous virgins.

My findings are that human life is morally and physically a mess and that the future is utterly unpredictable. Thus, true happiness lies in the ability to live with ambiguity, and the road to happiness runs along those paths through the dark wood that aren't blocked by the paralyzing blindness of ambivalence, or slicked to individual and collective idiocy by simplifications that can't bear the sunlight.

Earlier versions of parts of this book have appeared in *Descant*, on www.dooneyscafe.com, and in *The Heart Does Break: Canadian Writers on Grief and Mourning* by Jean Baird and George Bowering, Random House, 2009.

The quotes on pages 163 and 177 are from Sherwin B. Nuland, *How We Die: Reflections on Life's Final Chapter*, Vintage Books, New York, 1993, pages 168 and 169, respectively. The passage quoted from David Shields on page 9 is from *Reality Hunger: A Manifesto*, Alfred A. Knopf, New York, 2010, pages 25–26. The lyrics to "Little Things Mean a Lot" on page 169: words and music by Edith Lindeman and Carl Stutz, as recorded by Kitty Kallen in 1954.

*T*HE LAST TIME I TALKED to my mother, she announced that she hated my father. This was a couple of days before the end of November; she was in Penticton, B.C., and I was in Toronto. I'd called her on the telephone to ask about a recipe for Christmas cookies, but that wasn't really why I called. While I talked to her the week before I'd heard something odd in her voice, and I was checking to see if it had dissipated. It hadn't.

There's not a hell of a lot that's wise or comforting you can say to your mother when she drops a bomb like that. Particularly when she's 90 years old. You just let her speak her piece, and hope there are no more bombers taxiing down the runway. And of course, hating the man she'd been married to for 64 years wasn't the only thing she had on her mind. She'd spent the afternoon making the cookies I wanted the recipe for, she'd just packaged up a batch of beef stew into meal-sized portions for the freezer, and was about to start sewing the green net "Nanny Bags" of Christmas treats that had been a favourite of the small kids in the family since I'd been one of them. Did I think the kids still wanted them?

I assured her that they did, although I suspected, in a world filled with more spectacular confections, that they didn't care one way or another.

"Your father's supposed to be back from Kamloops any minute," she said, when I asked about him. That's when she dropped her bomb. "I can't say I'll be glad to see him. I think," (here was an auspicious pause as she considered what the right words should be) "I've finally gotten to the point where I *hate* him. He's your father, but I really just hate him. So there."

The flat finality of it was disturbing, but it didn't exactly take me by surprise. Things hadn't been going well between them for a long time, and to tell the truth, the rest of the family wasn't getting along much better.

We were, at that moment, on the verge of a civil war, with several fronts.

My father had recently delivered his voting shares in the family holding company to my older brother, Ron, and the three of us were snarling back and forth at one another across the new breach it opened. My twin sisters weren't getting along either, but their squabble, as always, was hard to read. They're identical twins who live 50 metres apart on Vancouver Island, and to them, everyone is an outsider. When they get going on one another, no one can really understand what it's about, let alone stop it.

I hadn't gotten along with my father since before I was a teenager, and my brother had serious issues with my mother, who, in typical fashion, had been arguing my case against my father with Ron about the voting shares, all the while telling *me* I ought to back off and let my brother take control because, for god's sake, he's earned the responsibility. She was trying to get both of us to chill out, but the way she'd been delivering the message was a little too emphatic to soothe either of us. So while it wasn't quite that the Fawcett family was holding one another at knifepoint, the knives were out, and the last several Family Reunions—annual events at which attendance wasn't optional—had been very tense.

For as long as anyone could remember, my father and mother had operated a domestic system with sharply demarcated spheres of influence and a strict division of labour. My father kept his fist firmly around the money, and after he retired, he gradually took over all the gardening, which lately involved mowing the grass at high speeds on his sit-down mower, planting exotic roses and spraying them with poisonous chemicals, growing beefsteak tomatoes the same way, and doing a lot of brutal pruning of his and his neighbours trees and shrubs to prevent any obscuring of his view of the Okanagan Valley, which he believed he had a God-given right to view, without obstruction, from his favourite chair in the living room.

My mother kept the house, which she ruled autocratically, most particularly the kitchen, where she was not to be trifled with, even though my sisters and I are equally skilled cooks. She also regulated and sometimes ruled our family life, although she did this with more subtlety and diplomacy than she displayed around the kitchen—or around my father, with whom she'd been engaged in an epic contest of wills since a few years after they were married.

Keeping this family running smoothly wasn't easy, given its size and the personalities involved. But now the toughest part of her job, since none of us lived close enough for day-to-day contact and mostly showed up at Christmas, Thanksgiving, or the Family Reunions, was my father. At his best, he'd never been easy to get along with, he hadn't mellowed with age, and in recent years, he was rarely at his best.

He was a man who cheated at cards, practised selective deafness so he wouldn't have to listen to anything he didn't want to hear, and regularly pissed off the neighbours by pruning their trees and shrubs without asking. Within the family, he had a long history of offering to lend money and then imposing humiliating conditions after the fact. He had a 35-year record of fomenting Darwinian contests between my brother and I whenever he got the opportunity, and this latest dust-up, was, well, just one of many. He did it, he said, to ensure the growth of his "business empire," which he'd cheerfully tell anyone, whether they'd asked or not, was the Most Important Thing in Life. I thought he did it to amuse himself, the bastard.

He also made a nuisance of himself at social gatherings by proselytizing right-wing political ideas barely this side of "shoot the poor," while trying to sell anyone who moved a foul-tasting dietary supplement called Barley Max, which he claimed could solve anyone's physical ills no matter what they were. When he got going, he'd claim that Barley Max could also cure his client-victims' spiritual and political shortcomings, which he was fond of pointing out to them in detail as part of the sales pitch.

Given that his eyesight was worse than his hearing and its badness wasn't at all selective, he was a public menace to everyone and everything whenever he got behind the wheel of his aging Cadillac Fleetwood. He was a still greater menace to the local newspaper's editor, to whom he wrote long grammar- and spelling-challenged letters about once a week, denouncing the government and whoever and whatever else he thought might be trying to screw with his business empire, or his right to scare the daylights out of unwary pedestrians and other drivers whenever they strayed into the path of his Cadillac.

The family picture wall, which ran 6 or 7 metres along one hallway wall in my parents' home, was probably the best evidence of the management difficulties my mother faced—and the way she dealt with those difficulties. It had been in flux since the first of my siblings reached puberty, and really, before even that. My father banished his father early in the marriage, and my mother, for different reasons, had banished hers. The wall grew more or less as you'd expect while my siblings and I were growing up: pictures of us in our sports teams and social groups, graduation photos, and so on. These photographs remained constant because they were, each of them, portraits of us the way she liked us best: young and if not exactly innocent, at least unscarred by experience.

When my sisters started bringing home their boyfriends, the wall began to grow. A couple of early boyfriends made it onto the wall, but were replaced by husbands by the time my sisters reached the age of 18. My brother's wives and then mine started going up a few years later. The grandchildren began to appear, and the wall grew still more.

Getting onto the wall, for outsiders, was easy. Tenure was another matter, as was staying married to any of us. A few legal spouses lasted several years, although one or two lasted only months before they offended my mother and were disappeared. The first ones were all replaced by new spouses or partners soon enough. The live-in boyfriends and girlfriends who replaced them made it onto the wall if my mother happened to like them. New wives and husbands, legal ones, were tolerated even when she didn't like them— until they in turn were replaced by later models, in which case they disappeared well before the divorce decrees were final. As the grandchildren grew up, they caused a further expansion of the wall, and their first partners were treated with careful democracy when my mother liked them, although a girlfriend of one of my nephews who'd yelled at several of us after we ran her beloved off the go-cart track during the family's annual takeover of the local facility at the Family Reunion had her picture taken down before the weekend was over. The nephew dropped her soon after.

The picture wall had been moved from house to house by my parents as they got older, and in their last house, a big single-level affair my father insisted would be his last building project, he gave the picture wall its own free-standing wall, a kind of in-family equivalent of the Kremlin's Hall of Glory. In that last house the wall grew considerably, partly because the family grew in size as great-grandchildren started to appear, but partly because there was space to be filled. It expanded, sure, but it was revised as much as it grew, always by my mother's increasingly capricious defenestrations. Despite these comings and goings, the wall's essential fuel remained the 14 divorces racked up by me, my brother, and my sisters.

While my mother and I chatted away that November evening, I thought about how diligently she'd kept the wall current, and I found myself wondering idly if she was now going to remove my father from it while he was still living in the house. But I didn't mention him again, and it wasn't very long before the emotional shorthand she and I had developed over the years reimposed the normalities she'd shattered. I copied down the cookie recipe—"Don't forget the nutmeg"—and I mentioned the idea I'd read somewhere about soaking the Christmas turkey in brine overnight before stuffing it, which she dismissed as silliness. She had her Christmas cards done and ready for mailing, and I told her I had, too, even though I hadn't started. We talked about some recent minor twinges she'd felt in her head over the last weeks, but said they were nothing. Then we talked about who was going where for Christmas, and then we were up to date. I assured her that everything would be all right, and she agreed that it of course would be, although that same odd note in her voice said otherwise. "I know it's all a big mess," she said, and sighed. "But family is important. I don't want this one to fall apart."

That was the last thing she said to me, ever. Two nights later, she suffered a major stroke that, among other things, rendered her unable to speak. Twelve days after that, she was dead.

April 1945

ONCE UPON A TIME, we were an ideal family. There were six of us: an industrious mother with a quick smile; a serious, hard-working father; twin girls; two younger boys, one—me—an infant. There were no health problems in this family, not a disability or cognitive delay reared its head, no troubling or unruly behaviours in the children were noted, and the parents had no debilitating vices or unattractive quirks. There was a tiny mortgage on the small home my father built by himself in a pleasant neighbourhood, there were mountains and rivers without end for the kids to roam through, and not a drop of non-British blood in our ancestry was admitted to—not that we cared who our ancestors were.

We were the kind of family that Canada's armed forces had just fought the Nazis and the Japanese to preserve, God Save the King. Now the war was ending, and the world, despite its convulsions, seemed as bright and filled with hope as at any point in human history. Penicillin had recently arrived to save us from bacteria, DDT would save us from disease-spreading crop-eating bugs; people like us knew nothing about the Holocaust, Hitler would be dead in a few weeks, Uncle Joe was still our friend, officially, anyway. The atomic bomb was still a few months in the future and we had no notion that the Cold War and the Communist Menace were being cooked up in the minds of American politicians and their military planners. An end to 30 years of misery and killing and maybe a beneficent World Government was what ordinary people could see on the horizon in April 1945.

It was a good time to be alive, and my parents knew it. There had been no war deaths in our extended family this time, and my father had the same secure job that had kept him from conscription. The photographs taken of us at the time show us clear-eyed, confident, and attractive: father in a business suit, mother in a comfortably fashionable housedress, and the four children dressed in clothes my mother had made herself. Each one of us gazes at the camera as if the world was someday going to belong to us. Picture-perfect; ideal.

But ideal, like picture-perfect, can be a long way from perfection. Even the picture, examined more closely, reveals some flaws. We are posed on the whitewashed porch of the white clapboard house my father had just built. The porch, if you look, needs several more coats of whitewash, and you can't see that the house behind us is cold in winter because the sawdust that fills its walls for insulation is already settling. The part of the world we inhabit has a few flaws, too: a small dirty frontier town called Prince George, B.C., set at the confluence of the blue Nechako and muddy Fraser rivers, and surrounded by limitless forests of pine and spruce trees at the then-northern limit of settled Canada. We are isolated from our extended families and most of the amenities bigger cities offered in those days. The northern winters are very cold and snow-filled, the roads uncertain most of the year—or non-existent—and food, although plentiful enough, is sharply limited in variety due to the transport distances.

To my parents, Hartley Fawcett and Rita Surry, these less-than-perfect things are acceptable trade-offs for the freedoms they gain by living on the frontier. My father is free of his destiny, that of a subsistence grain farmer, and my mother is free of her own troubled family. They can look to the future, which they believe *will* be perfect. My father, always an optimist, believes that Prince George will be populated with a million people by the twenty-first century, and he has nearly a million plans to get his share of the wealth all that growth and progress is going to bring. My mother likes the town, too, but for different reasons. "I knew from the first moment," she will tell me years later, "that this would be a safe place to raise my children."

This is as good a place as any to warn you that this book is a memoir, and that, even though I wasn't a particularly loyal or attentive son to my parents, I have a familial as well as authorial stake in it. I'm very much aware of what the incendiary American cultural critic David Shields recently wrote: "We remember what suits us, and there's almost no limit to what we can forget. Only those who keep faithful diaries will know what they were doing at this time, on this day, a year ago. The rest of us recall only the most intense moments, and even these tend to have been mythologized by repetition into well-wrought chapters in the story of our lives. To this extent, memoirs really can claim to be modern novels, all the way down to the presence of an unreliable narrator."

It happens that I have a fairly odd sort of memory, insofar as I seem to go quite far out of my way to *not* remember the intense moments that families tend to mythologize. What I do have recall on, and with an unsettling degree of clarity, are the moments of physical slapstick that are part of everyone's life, and usually a suppressed part. I inherited both my mother's bullshit detector, which was the most extraordinary piece of equipment life conferred on her, and my father's inability to suffer fools quietly even when I'm the fool. I also have, thanks to modern digital photography, an unusually large collection of family photographs, along with a trick that has helped me to penetrate their surfaces: I enlarge them to 8 1/2 x 11, which lets me peruse them at a level of detail not previously available. You saw one small result a moment ago when I pointed out the poor whitewash job on the steps in the 1945 family portrait. And at the risk of seeming immodest, I am a skilled researcher, and an obsessive amateur detective. Finally, I am hyper-aware of the dangers of what I'm doing, and not, in the normal course of things, prone to getting washed overboard by sentimentality.

What I'm trying to figure out here, as the title of the book suggests, is what human happiness is about, and what it tells us. I'm examining it through the lens of the happiness my parents felt at being in the world. I want to discover what specific cultural or personal tools they used to build and maintain it, and where that tool box went. Because the tool box has vanished, and what makes human beings happy has changed.

When Hartley Fawcett and Rita Surry were young, happiness was a noble pursuit, one that, in their minds, led without ambivalence to "the Good Life." But somewhere in the last half century, "the Good Life" has lost its definite article. Today, one can only lead *a* good life, and that has become an ideological, censorious, and antihumanist term, one that can be experienced only individually. Not sure what I'm talking about?

Try to imagine a group of people gathering on a contemporary North American or European civic space to celebrate the joys and achievements of humanity. First of all, it isn't going to happen. If it did, it would draw a hostile counter-demonstration: animal rights activists who'd argue that we're mistreating every other species; environmentalists, most of whom see human beings as a terrible scourge on everything else on the planet, would join in, followed by anti-racists hollering that all this fun is coming at the expense of the underdeveloped nations and people of colour, wherever they're living; supporters of NGOs dedicated to wiping out disease and poverty in the underdeveloped world would join in, bickering at the celebrants for not doing enough, not doing more.

I remember my mother, while I was very young, excusing the weakness of a family friend by saying, well, she's only human. It was a forgiving, affectionate explanation, and I recognized that at its root was the idea that to be *only human* was an essentially good thing. I was comforted by the thought that I too was only human.

But somewhere along the line, that comfort has vanished. To be "only human" in the twenty-first century is to be *merely* human, an aggressive and distasteful condition. It means being disconnected from nature's laws, it means being selfishly venal, and probably destructive: an alien force, hostile to the well-being of the planet, at the bottom of the hierarchy of goodness.

How did we get to this? I and my children may end up leading good lives, but we have no shot at the Good Life the way my parents understood it because our joy and comfort at being what we are comes at the expense of one of a thousand disadvantaged minorities or will contribute to the further impoverishment of fragile landscapes and ecosystems, will endanger every threatened animal or plant, and will further pollute the planet. I can live with this because I'm used to it. But my kids have lost their right to collective human happiness because it is too costly to the planet and to the rest of their fellow human beings. That bothers me. It leaves them to lead guilty lives, with pleasures that are deemed anti-social and selfish.

Something else. The empirical observer in me has noticed that most people today think about happiness the same way art critics see still life painting: as a fixed state in which a nexus of static objects supposedly sheds an aura of light and exactness that evokes a summarizing kind of external meaning, usually in the form of a slogan. Life Is Short; Life Is Beautiful; Pleasure Is Fleeting; Don't Worry, Be Happy.

At its core, still life is a distortion. If it were language, it would make sentences in which there are only nouns, with a halo of sepia where the verbs ought to be. Inside that sepia, however, rests the creator's slogan, along with whatever prejudices he or she may have about the world. In art, and sometimes in life, there are formal intentions which take the form of a prescriptive syntax. For instance, some of the objects in a still life must be of human fabrication, some must be harvested from the world. In a typical still life, you might find a dead pheasant resting beside a rotting pear lying in front of an old bottle, while across the pheasant's breast lies a slightly rusted knife.

The contemplation of still life constructions comforts people, but I don't believe them for a moment. There is no such thing as still life, not really. Life is never still. The pear will soon rot or be eaten, the dead pheasant must be plucked and put into a hot oven before the maggots take over, the bottle recycled in a blue box or filled with gasoline and stuffed with a rag to make a Molotov cocktail. Don't ask about the knife. And then there's the *real world*, the one most of us live in day by day trying to find happiness—or a car dealership that gives away BMWs.

Happiness is subject to the same logic as still life: in the real world, if happiness and/or still life or even the Good Life exists, it is only for a moment, and glimpsed in flight. Things *must* move along in the real world, and every attempt to control or stop the movement fuels the slapstick that breaks it down into the human condition: moments after the painter sets his (or her) arrangement, his spouse (or one-eyed hunchbacked assistant) trips over a bucket of apples or empty Pepsi cans and scatters the arrangement. The bottle smashes on the floor, the family dog grabs the pheasant and runs for the door, trailed by the screeching spouse and followed, at a more leisurely pace, by the painter, who has a slight smile because he (or she) understands the artifice of the still life arrangement and the ease of making another construction—or maybe there is a lover waiting a few blocks away, and this accident will hasten the end of the working day.

Real world happiness isn't, as the pie-faced optimists of Oprah Winfrey's reality have it, an arrangement of self-inflating, easily faked pieties and on-camera revelations. It is intangible and limited, a fleetingly experienced emotional evanescence lodged within a continuum of other, not-necessarily-sanguine events. Except for a few very underemployed, self-involved, or very lucky people, happiness isn't an accomplishment one gets to flash like a police badge or a designer handbag. It moves and shifts within the currents of everything else, always elusive, rarely surfacing in the same way or in the same figuration. Without effort, attitude, and concentration you don't even know that it's there, and even if you do, you're more likely to trip over it and fall down the stairs than to find the time to clasp it to your spiritual bosom and genuflect over it.

But wait! The photograph of my family, taken in April 1945, rebukes this. The postures and characters you see in it—and the strain of happiness it self-consciously attempts to represent—remained still and stable until the twenty-first century, more or less. On the left is my sister Serena, named by my father before he knew he had twins, and given the name for her demeanour at birth.

He holds her, not quite closely, both of them gazing at the camera as if the eye of the future was upon them. Behind him my brother, Ron, stands, a little shy, but proud to be at his father's shoulder. I'm on my mother's knee, chubby and imperious, the little prince on his throne. My mother's smile is like my brother's, shy but determined all the same. On my mother's left is Nina, Serena's older-by-a-half-hour twin, not serene at all. She is coiled and impish; full of light. Ideal, picture-perfect happiness.

It took my mother's death to shake us from these ideal stances. By then, we were anything but picture-perfect.

An Authorial Intrusion

$\mathcal{I}$F THE STORY HERE was a novel, it would want to be a bittersweet tale about a marriage that didn't make anyone happy, lightened and elevated by how the lovers struggled to be happy by different means. I'd call it *The Good Life*, or something even sillier, and paint it by numbers into symmetries as phony as they would be picturesque. But this isn't a novel, and I'll explain exactly why it can't be.

A few weeks ago, on the way back from a family funeral, this time on my wife's side, I stopped at a supermarket to buy a carton of light cream for the coffee drinkers who were coming over to commiserate. As I pulled my car off the road and glided through the supermarket's parking lot, I was thinking, not of the immediate family death, but that of a close friend I went to high school with who'd recently died of a heart attack after 40 years trapped inside a schizophrenic fog. I pulled up beside a green minivan, and sat for a moment, lost in thought, tears rolling down my cheeks.

But an odd sound was coming from the minivan, and when I looked over, there was a 5-pound Chihuahua plastered against the driver's-side window, snarling and splattering the window with drool as it tried to chew its way through the glass to get at me. As far as this mutt was concerned, I was Adolf Hitler and the Communist Menace rolled into one, and if I came near his property and even if not, well . . .

Crazed Chihuahuas that interrupt theme-based reveries just aren't found in novels. In my world, they're the everyday ciphers I navigate with.

So, I'll spin you the love story I found, and I'll do my best to make sense of the struggles of the main characters, whose lives, now over, were about equally filled with love and conflict. But both immediately and ultimately, this is as much rooted in slapstick as in romance or grim mortality: comedy is the unacknowledged third element that human life is constructed from.

I also have other ambitions for this. The serious part of me wants to uncover what two unambitious lives reveal about our dead-in-the-water civilization, where history and progress have broken and we are all off chasing private entitlements and BMWs and investment portfolios on a planet with dwindling resources, overburdened infrastructure and a rapidly faltering natural environment. We have too many of one species—ours, not those cattle farting in the meadow—and now we're breaking up into a myriad of factions and tribes, most of them bristling with weapons, the hand-held automatic kind, and the larger ones, the WMDs that George Bush's America couldn't find in Iraq because the industrialized oligarchies of the Cold War have them all. That's the mess we've made of the bright future we inherited from the rubble of the Second World War, and I won't remind you of it again because there's no need to. Everyone knows that the world is a mess, and it scares the hell out of most of us, me included. By the end of their lives, the main characters in this narrative knew it was a mess, too. Over their lifetime, its undertow grabbed at their resolve like it does yours and mine, and they could almost, but not quite, hear the rumble of the missile silos at the margins of some of their conversations, not much differently than I heard them for 30 years of my life. It was a kind of "black noise" at the bottom of everything in the last half of the twentieth century, and it darkened the slapstick as much as the high drama, birthing a new strain of gallows humour on a global scale. This black noise is less recognized but more affective than the white noise that is technology's constant signature in our doings.

Look at it this way: the three most influential public figures of the twentieth century, Adolf Hitler, Joseph Stalin, and Mao Zedong, ordered—sometimes directly—the deaths of about 35 million people, and were indirectly responsible for 40 or 50 million more. No instrument can accurately calculate the pain and misery that these and a depressingly long list of other "exemplary" people have spread, and no language can articulate the affront to life itself those wasted or prematurely terminated lives constitute.

This is therefore unapologetically a narrative about how some ordinary people made their way through a world that changed much more than they did, and about how they adapted—or didn't. It will be an account of cruelties and kindnesses, commitment and broken commitments, stupidity and wisdom, cunning and obliviousness, selfishness and sacrifice: the human condition, lower case, and close up.

Am I making everything sound bleak? It wasn't. Not for them, and not for anyone who came in contact with them. And that brings me to my other ambition for this story, which is that, despite all the grim darkness that surrounds us, my parents' lives were filled with life-affirming decencies and sweet, comedic interludes. Small, decent lives like the ones in this book might be the best accomplishments of the twentieth century. These were people who lived without violence, people who ignored the vaunted programmatic ideologies that shattered nations and laid waste to entire continents. They lived with grounded common sense, which they exercised without causing notable harm or displacement to anyone, including themselves, and they stumbled and fell a lot while they were exercising, almost as if they were reminding themselves of how inexact the instruments they had to work with were.

My mother, one of the two primary players in this comedy, lived her entire nine decades within the century she was born in, always distant from the furnaces of violence. She lived her life without spectacular ambitions or accomplishments. But what she did do during her life was create more laughter than misery, and she was capable of outbursts of brilliant, calming happiness that she recognized and learned to articulate so that others could be warmed and illuminated by it. Some of us were, when we weren't stumbling around and tripping over things and otherwise getting mired in the mess.

My father, who spent nearly 93 of his 100 years in the twentieth century, had, well, a thorough if often selfish good time. Then— not to give the punchline of this entire affair away—he spent his last eight years making whatever restitution was needed, and in the process, changed himself and everyone who was close to him.

There's something else that makes all this worth the telling: the two central figures in this story literally couldn't have imagined that a story could be written about their lives. They both had the sort of modesty of expectation that prevented them from seeing themselves as central to anything, even, at times, their own lives. They didn't see their marriage as drama, or their lives as a narrative that had a fireworks-and-orchestra beginning followed by plot-point catastrophes and epiphanies, and they didn't see its ending coming until it was on them even though they both prepared for death in exquisite detail. They saw their individual lives and their marriage through the lens of *a plan*, one that they pursued relentlessly without talking about it very much, and except in moments they thought of as weakness, without looking back to see what had worked and what hadn't.

This is also about the *desire* to find a human and humane happiness, about the goodness of the human spirit, about the unappreciated comedy of our expectations and it is about the will we don't hear very much about these days. Not the will to dominate others, or make life about ourselves, but the often-interrupted will to love and be loved, and the contagious decency that arises from it.

My private motives? Like most people born in North America during and just after the Second World War, I grew up without the faintest curiosity about the people who'd brought me into the world, and even less about the ancestors who had gotten them to our staging grounds. Toward the end of my parents' lives I began to understand that this lack of curiosity was a serious mistake, and in part, this book is my attempt at restitution: this is about them, but it is also for them.

The Sociological Script

I N 1945, my parents' marriage, then in its tenth year, was as troubled as it was solid. My father, who'd been forced to quit school in the seventh grade when he left home, had a first-rate brain, courage, and an eye for making money. He'd worked his way from the delivery trucks of a meat-packing company to travelling salesman, and by the end of the war he held the largest territory his company covered, and was looking for other ways to build up enough capital to buy a business of his own. Within the definitions acceptable at the time, he was an excellent provider, and a capable if emotionally limited parent and husband. My mother suffered from mild bouts of depression even though that wasn't a recognized affliction at the time, socially or clinically, and she harboured profound resentments toward my father. Some were private and specific, some were generic enough that they might have been found in a sociology textbook 25 years later.

Part of the conflict between them *was* larger than they were. It was the product of the Second World War. Yes, the war lifted North American women's horizons. But it had made their men heroic, whether they'd been soldiers or not. In 1945, unless you'd spent the war in a jail or under a rock, you were a hero, man or woman.

Everyone's sightlines were elevated. The just and logical gender goals of women like my mother were soon enough cancelled out by the elevated personal outlook—mostly aimed at business goals—of men like my father. This served to turn postwar domestic life, for many married couples, into small, intense contests of will and barely perceptible wars of attrition.

Yet sociology depersonalizes too much. To my mother, her situation didn't feel like a bloodless element in a statistical formula. Her circumstances were oppressive, and she was distressed by them. By the beginning of the 1940s, she had birthed three children within 18 months of one another, and then she'd had to care for them with little help from my father. She felt abandoned by the man with whom she had chosen to make a life, and she was angry at him—angry enough to have gotten pregnant without his consent, and initially, at least, against his will. She had the right, and she exercised it, but even a fourth child, one she had time to enjoy, hadn't cooled the anger. It was there, an undertow hidden in the calm currents of their outwardly happy life. Months and sometimes years passed without its poisonous stream reaching the surface. Yet it was there, and it would remain.

Let me try to disentangle this back eddy with a very specific vignette, one without a shred of slapstick in it. My father, in the spring of 1940, returned home late one Friday night after a week of selling on the muddy roads of mid-eastern Alberta. The next morning, he ate a hearty breakfast that my mother made for him, and then took off for the day to play golf with some business friends.

They'd only recently moved to Camrose, then a dusty farming town 80 kilometres southeast of Edmonton. They'd been married in Edmonton in 1936 and both of them had spent most of their adult lives in that city. My mother knew no one in Camrose, and she had, with little domestic help or adult companionship, three children under the age of 2 1/2: my twin sisters, born in April

1938, and my brother, born in October 1939. She wasn't used to the isolation, and she found herself carrying a domestic load that was heavy and more than a little frightening.

Try to imagine the exchange between the two of them when he returned from the links late that afternoon.

Or rather, don't, because it will be very unpleasant. It would begin with a young, overtired wife bickering at a young, self-involved husband who doesn't think domestic duties, even the kind that involve very young offspring he is proud to have fathered, are his responsibility. This is the primary marital tableau of the last 70 years in Western countries, the one that produced feminism, radical feminism, millions of divorces, and uncountable hours of squalor and misery, personal, marital, and civil.

These two were civilized people, so the exchange would not have featured histrionics. No dishes would have been thrown, no one tore out their hair, no doors were slammed. My mother would likely have sulked for several hours, my father might have asked what was wrong, and she might have tried to explain, with some sharpness in her voice, that she was exhausted by the children and anxious about the isolation; not having family close by for company and help, not having close friends for companionship while he was out and about. For god's sake, Hartley.

My father might have offered a half-hearted apology, swiftly followed by an excuse: he worked hard all week, he needed to unwind, and the Golf Club was a place to meet the local businessmen—for him, actual or potential customers. Privately he would have shrugged it off: women are high-strung, lazy, prone to be controlling—this last item was to become a lifelong theme for him. But also this. Since he knew better, he'd go golfing again next week if the weather was good. Customers to talk with, relaxing to be done. He was in charge, he was a man of his time.

My mother's case is stronger, but only through twenty-first-century eyes. For their time and locale, neither is decisively wrong or right. Most domestic wars start here, with missed signals, lazy self-regard, and the absence of evil intentions. But the wars start anyway, and before long few combatants can remember what is was that touched off the fighting or what, exactly, they're fighting for. But the wounds are inflicted, they bleed and fester, and half a century and then some passes in a flash.

My mother was vulnerable and alone, and for her, there was nothing abstract about it. She did not sense any sociological currents moving around her, did not imagine that she was a part of any groundbreaking movement, and she had no revolutionary zeal. There were the long days with only the demanding company of her three toddlers, and the longer nights in the chilly little house in a cold bed. She kept things together: stoked the wood furnace, did the wash on the primitive washboard and tub, and she fed wood and coal into the stove in the kitchen. In the winter she shovelled the snow from the sidewalks, bundled up her babies and took them out into the flat and windy streets, nursed them through the croup and the mumps and whooping cough, always alone. She'd been abandoned, and she experienced the crushing loneliness of this, along with small eddies of fear that it was a loneliness that wasn't going to be temporary. She stared at the wall, gazed out the kitchen window, didn't read novels because they made her feel disoriented and separated from her children, the ones she couldn't bear to be parted from even for a few hours. What could she do about her isolation?

She was resourceful, and not shy. There were other women's husbands out on the links with hers, weren't there? Wouldn't they feel as she did, that things weren't right? She knocked on her neighbours' doors, told them who she was, and then cultivated the ones she liked, the ones who shared her situation, building a small community for herself. She joined the local Women's Institute, found that most were farmers' wives, more likely to be beaten up for bickering than left alone. On the radio one morning, after the radio soap *Laura of Laura Limited* ("a woman," the show's announcer explained each morning, "who lived by the dictates of her own heart"), she heard about a newfangled women's organization called Beta Sigma Phi, which had recently formed an inaugural chapter in Edmonton. Several months later she started a chapter of her own in Camrose and when the family moved to Prince George in 1943, she started another. She wasn't trying to change the world, but she did sweeten her life a little, and it gave a backhanded confirmation of the anger she harboured: women's lives were hard even though they were safe and secure and the future was bright and about to be filled with washing machines and electric stoves and gas furnaces. But those bleak Monday mornings remained bleak, and the nights remained lonely.

I don't think my father ever quite understood why his wife was angry or how deep the anger ran. But after five years of intermittent hostility and a move to a town still more isolated than Camrose, he began, slowly, to tune out domestic life and to focus his prodigious energies on the business opportunities that would enable him to make his fortune. He'd be what his wife once told her father she was marrying for: a good provider who promised to have her, one day, riding in a Cadillac.

Be careful what you wish for, I guess.

Neither of these people were dreamers. They didn't wish they could wear velvet coats and go to the symphony. They were practical people with goals, focused on financial security and social success, not on culture or personal achievements, of which there was little to be had anyway. For them, their children's education was an obligation, a means to an end, nothing more. I don't think they imagined any of their children going beyond high school before going into the business world to make fortunes of their own.

After 1945 the years passed, some slowly, some momentous and swift. The ideal children grew, the ideal parents grew older. Quirks grew into fixations and neuroses, and some of their disappointments into grudges and phobias. The sunny future of Hartley Fawcett and Rita Surry turned into a stream of present days and nights that bore no resemblance to a fairy tale. The backlighting was dim and the orchestra didn't play at all. Everything changed, and nothing did. Dreams submerged beneath the twisting currents of the world, altered and scarred by time, fouled with the debris of daily life. Rough beasts slouched across the landscape, going nowhere. The centre didn't disintegrate, but it was often hard to locate.

Don't get me wrong. Most days, they were cheerful and engaged, and focused on their goals. Like the majority of people lucky enough to have lived in North America in the last century, they experienced real-world happiness as a common occurrence. It was as common as oxygen, nearly as invisible, and almost as crucial to survival.

That makes them very different from their ancestors. In the deep past, my parents' parents and more distant ancestors had spent their lives trying to keep their heads above the murky water, trying to get themselves free of other people's treadmills, too busy surviving to offer the past a goodbye or the future much more than a shrug toward the horizon as they left to work the fields. My parents could see a brighter future than that, and were wholly focused on getting to it. They didn't have a sense of either continuity or history because they had broken with the past and with the way people had done things in the past: families that exploited or abused one another, soldiers who had killed one another, bosses who put their boots on your neck and pushed your face in the mud, countries that invaded one another or dropped bombs on peaceful cities. That was over, and they were determined to leave it behind. Yet they didn't see themselves as exemplary or heroic. They were ordinary people working their way toward a better future. Their world was a bright place, the future brighter still, and they were content to be who they were, and where they lived. But the sun doesn't shine every day.

In the future they got, many things got better for them. My mother got her appliances, there was less drudgery for her, her children all grew up and married and had children of their own. Some of her wishes were fulfilled, most of my father's were, but some of the things they wanted proved impossible or empty or preposterous. Gradually, the ideal family of 1945 descended into nuance and an ordinariness that brought pain to both my parents in different ways. The city my father predicted would have a million citizens at the millennium had barely 100,000 at the beginning of the twenty-first century, its forests depleted by logging and self-inflicted ecological catastrophe; its wealth stolen by the corporations or merely squandered; crime was rampant; and the city was losing population daily.

Imagine these two people on a wide river, not as flotsam, yet not as smug boaters on a Sunday lake. They see the river's restless power clearly, its currents and eddies, and they accept that rapids and whirlpools might lie ahead, even though they have no deep expectations about absolute or final destinations, spiritual or tangible. Imagine them in a small blue boat drifting downstream. They are looking for ways to move their boat here and there, side to side— not to get to the shore but to avoid the hazards of the currents, and to take advantage of them. My mother leans over the water, sculling distractedly. My father sits upright, scanning the river for the means to devise a paddle—or better still, a set of oars so they can ply the currents together. It is April 1945. And, in the blink of an eye, it is December 2000.

Wild Strawberries

HARTLEY FAWCETT fervently believed that he was a self-created man, and Rita Surry, just as passionately if not as loudly, molded herself and her life as the exception to every rule by which her family lived—or, in her view, ran amok. That made them both, like their own parents and immediate ancestors and unlike their siblings, pioneers. Pioneers are unrooted people, interested in acquiring property, making money, and building large families as a protection against old age and contingency. They are contemptuous of the past, oblivious to most cultural and historical nuance and indifferent toward anything other than practical understanding.

But my parents were a different sort of pioneer: less constrained by subsistence, and the frontier they sought was as much psychological as it was physical. They wanted to get ahead of other people, build solid material foundations for the future, and, most important of all, do things differently than their parents and siblings.

Pioneers are different from immigrants. My wife's Eastern European parents, although born in North America, are typical of immigrants in that they are most interested in family and ethnic solidarity, educating their children and gaining social prestige. They have been obsessed by questions of obligation and social responsibility that held little interest for either of my parents.

Me? I'm Canadian, which is different again. I have a sensibility that includes elements of both pioneer and immigrant values, but has been shaped by the multicultural society around me. I'm trying hard, for instance, to infect my children with a sense of their genetic and social connectedness to both the people around them *and* to their ancestors, and I'd like them to have a deeper appreciation of the complexity of the present and past than I was brought up to observe. But like my parents before me, I have no ethnic chauvinisms, and I have their determination to do things my own way, their eye for practicalities, and I have their skeptical view of social convention: if everyone is doing it, that is cause for wariness.

Put another way, I want my children to understand the specific flavour of wild strawberries and I want them to know where to look for them. I want them to know how wild strawberries differ from the genetically modified and tasteless agribusiness strains, and in which ways—and when—the flavour of the local strawberries in season still resembles the wild ones.

Being Canadian this way, and with an almost infinitely better access to the specifics of the past provided by an information-enriched world, has convinced me that the people who raised me weren't *entirely* self-created. Like most people, their family histories reveal more than a few things they couldn't—or wouldn't—have: the contrariness of their characters, why they got so far from home and from their families and the comforts offered. That's why I've located the family closet, and have pried open its door. Out pour the skeletons—and the wild strawberries.

The wild strawberries I'll pick and try to present with their flavour intact. The skeletons are another matter: they explain too many of the *whys* and *whats* to leave out, but they're not the story, which is about two people who deliberately stepped outside the slow-moving continuums of history and genetics that made them. Thus, I've forced the skeletons back into the closet, and I've parked the closet at the end of the book, for the edification of those who want to open it.

How my parents first met isn't a story that has survived in the form of a singular thrilling anecdote. Hartley Fawcett worked on the trucks for a meat-packing company and Rita Surry worked at the Hudson's Bay Company, the largest meat and grocery outlet in Edmonton at the time, so it seems logical to suppose that she met him that way.

But maybe not. My mother once told me a wistful story about my father appearing at one of the dances she organized with her girlfriends. He'd been the date of an acquaintance, and she herself was there with a police constable she didn't much fancy. She spotted my father the moment he walked in, and said that he spent the evening glancing at her. He was slim, handsome, and strongly built, with bright hazel eyes and a shock of jet-black hair. She said he had a reputation for wildness, but quickly added that what mattered to

her was that he was a man with strength and ambition, and that his wildness could be tamed.

"He was a catch," she said, ruefully. "But when you're in love, you can't really be sure of exactly what kind of fish you're catching."

Fred Surry, my mother's father, ran across my father well before she did. Hartley Fawcett had shown up at the taxi stand next door to Fred's book and coin shop to collect whatever he could of the thousand dollars he'd lent to one of the taxi owners, a burly pipe smoker in his late thirties.

When the cabbie didn't have the money he owed and showed no inclination to get and give it up, an argument ensued. Fred Surry heard the commotion, and arrived too late to catch the taxi owner taking the first swing at my father. But he was *perfectly* timed to see my father counter with a punch that put the larger man's pipe through the side of his left cheek—and to then watch my father stand over him as he bled and threaten to do worse if he didn't pay up, and soon.

The impression Fred Surry got from the incident was almost as inaccurate as it was dramatic. Hartley Fawcett was no thug and he wasn't one to start fights. He just ended them, usually with a punch-line. What Fred had seen was a young man convinced of his cause—the latter trait would be a lifelong constant—and a counter-puncher able to back up his cause with a boxer's right hand and a mouth to match.

That first impression was the only one Fred Surry was willing to entertain, and my father did nothing to alter it. When Fred found out his daughter was dating him, he tried to stop it, cornering my father when he brought her home at midnight from their first date.

"Just what do you think you've been doing with my daughter until this time of night?" he screeched.

"Out chasing chickens," my father snapped back, likely sensing that he was doomed no matter what he said. "Be thankful I've brought her home at all."

My mother kept dating him over her father's objections. It isn't clear if he kept her out all night before they were married, but there were tales about motorcycle rambles deep into the Alberta country-side, and others about sleeping in haystacks. There's also a rumour that the two of them rode his big motorcycle to Vancouver and back. That hints at many things, not the least of which is that my mother's youthful stamina and her zest for adventure weren't so different from my father's. In the early 1930s, Vancouver to Edmonton was a round trip of almost 3000 kilometres, and over roads too stony and bad to even think about.

When my parents married in August 1936, Fred Surry refused to attend the ceremony. He forbade my grandmother to go, too, but she went anyway, to hell with you. After that, he refused to be in the same room with his son-in-law and went so far as to disinherit my mother in a 1937 revision of his will. He called my father "the Indian"—it was unclear if he was referring to the motorcycle or his dark good looks—and predicted future moral and financial doom for his eldest daughter.

There's no question that my parents were in love when they married, but there was a calculated element on both sides. It's clear that to my father, Rita Surry was a "catch": she was pretty if not quite beautiful; she was sensible and practical, and very organized and focused. She was better educated than he was, more cultured, and more socially adept. For her, he was a project, and of course, also a "catch": handsome, strong, and ambitious, a man with the sort of inner drive that she sensed could be molded. My mother didn't stray far from her common sense, even in matters of love. Romance was one thing, but as the saying goes, *you gotta have something in the bank, Frank*. She did not want to be poor the way her parents had been, and my father promised her that one day, she would ride in Cadillacs.

So there was romance, and love, and there was marriage, and the future, on which and in which they would work together. That was the deal; that was the ground of their love for one another.

*   *   *

Now, I believe that all marriages begin with a fund of goodwill that, once spent, is difficult to regenerate. If there is too much inattention or lying or if there is infidelity in a marriage, it devours a portion of the goodwill that can't be regenerated. The marriage might survive—less frequently today than in past generations—but it will do so with reduced passion, and commensurately decreased trust.

As husbands go, my father had strong virtues. He was financially responsible, he didn't drink or gamble or hang out with the guys unless it was business, and he didn't chase around, come home late or not at all. He was a man focused on financial security and on business success, he saved money, and was unusually competent at the things husbands of his era needed to be good at: he could bang boards together, fix anything around the house, and he was a genius with mechanical devices. What more could a wife ask for?

Quite a lot. By nature, my father wasn't a physically affectionate man, although he seems to have tried to be during the first years of the marriage. According to my mother, he was a clumsy and inattentive lover who grew less attentive as he got older. He also carried never-to-be-examined beliefs that men were superior to their women and that he had to be the boss. Even in the last months of his long life, he still hadn't wavered on either.

In the 1930s and 1940s his shortcomings were hardly villainous, and they certainly weren't unusual. But to my mother, they caused frustrations, irritations, disappointments that chipped away at both her self-respect and her affection for him. But she had settled *on* my father as well as settled *for* him, and that was not something that ever really occurred to her to reconsider. Yet she wanted a good marriage, and that meant good in the less tangible ways too: she believed, well before its time, that sexual happiness was her right. And so, subtly and unconsciously as the goodwill between them began to dissipate, she turned away from him, shifting her focus to her children, and my father's focus shifted to business—getting her that Cadillac he'd promised her.

Understanding my father's perspective is more difficult because he was, as most men are, less articulate about what he wanted from his wife and from marriage. I think he got most of what he wanted: a competent homemaker, a healthy mother for his children, one who cared for them as they grew up. In my mother he also got a couple of bonuses he likely found useful without being able to admit it. He got a wife with the social graces he lacked, and one with a better head for figures than he possessed. She kept the family books until she was in her mid-eighties, and during the 1950s when his business was touch-and-go, she kept her finger atop the accounts.

But what didn't he get? I can hear my mother's snorted answer: "Someone who'd take his bloody orders without questioning them. And it's a good thing I didn't take his orders. He'd have put us in the poorhouse several times with his stupid schemes."

That's not wrong, but it isn't complete. He didn't get much sweet goodwill from my mother, either, not that he'd earned it. And so he lived without it, just as she did. The marriage went on, always a functioning partnership, but it was not the stuff of sweet dreams. My mother rode in the Cadillac, eventually. But she never once got to drive the damned thing. Not even after she'd had a driver's licence for 40 years.

And so the years begin to pass. My father quits his safe job, buys his business and begins to work 14 hours a day. My sisters grow into teenagers, get pregnant and are both married by 18, my older brother buys his first car and I don't make the Little League all-star team. I do acquire a star-shaped scar on my forehead, which I earn by filling a small jam jar with gunpowder I collect by taking a knife and screwdriver to my father's shotgun ammunition, poking a firecracker fuse through the jam jar's lid, lighting the fuse, and then standing in a circle with my friends to watch the explosion from

3 metres away. A shard of glass nails me in the forehead hard enough to knock me cold for a few seconds, and my closest friend catches another shard in his leg just below the knee. Two weeks later, he and I will blow up his mother's concrete washtubs with gunpowder we've manufactured from scratch.

In other people's lives, a second railroad arrives in Prince George; politicians deposit tons of bullshit about all the wealth the railroad will bring when most of what it brought were empty railcars to haul away the trees and hungry people looking for jobs. A P-38 Lightning crashes into the sandbanks across the river at 500 kilometres per hour after buzzing the main street of town at 30 metres; the city's population doubles, the roads improve and pavement multiplies; my father's business prospers; and trees, many trees, come down. Life in northern British Columbia, in other words, is normal.

Breast Cancer

IN THE SUMMER of 1960, a few months after my parents returned from three weeks travelling in Europe because my father had won a North American sales prize for selling Pepsi-Cola, my mother found a hard lump in her left breast. Having been warned, even in those distant days, what the lump might be, she booked an appointment with our family doctor, a man named Peter Jaron I remember mainly for having skin rashes on his neck and hands. In a leisurely sort of way, Dr. Jaron arranged for a biopsy, and about a month later called my mother on the phone just as I was arriving home from school. The biopsy, he told her, "was positive."

"Positive?" I hear her say, with such careful calm that I should have been instantly alert. "What do you mean by positive?"

Peter Jaron's answer is equally calm. "The growth in your breast is malignant. You have breast cancer. You should come in sometime this week, so we can get the process going."

"Process?" my mother asks, disturbed by Jaron's matter-of-fact tone. "What process are we talking about? The process of dying?"

"The treatment process. There's some urgency about this," Jaron admits.

"When can I come in?" she says.

There is some fumbling at the other end of the line. "Let me see when I've got an open spot."

My mother slams down the phone, and bursts into tears. I ask her what is wrong. "Nothing," she says, gathering herself together. "I'll be fine."

Satisfied, I wander downstairs to my bedroom, close the door, and begin to work on the 1/25th scale model car I've been customizing, a late-model Ford I've painstakingly decorated with several coats of maroon candy-apple paint. It looks fine.

But my mother isn't fine, and over the next several days, she does something about it. She contacts a family friend, Larry Maxwell, a doctor who has recently taken a sabbatical from the local hospital to improve his oncological expertise. He agrees to take her on as a patient, and the worst three years of her life begin.

There are several things about the above tableau you should know. The first is that it is a fabrication drawn from the wispiest shreds of fact and memory. When this reconstruction started, I had just three ciphers to work with, other than the knowledge that my mother contracted breast cancer and underwent a radical mastectomy of her left breast at some point between 1956 and 1966. I had to call my sister Nina to get the dates straight, and we were able to pinpoint 1960 by cross-referencing events in Nina's life: the breakup of her first marriage, and the subsequent year she and her infant daughter spent living with my parents. It took us a while to sort out the few certainties we could muster between us.

One of the certain ciphers is a memory fragment of mine in which my mother is telling me that I will be going to a new doctor.

"Why is that?" I asked.

She grimaced. "I don't think," she said, choosing her words deliberately the way she did when something was difficult, "that Dr. Jaron pays proper attention to his patients."

The thought of having a new doctor interested me. But maybe it was that I didn't like Jaron's skin rashes and the fact that his arms and neck were coated with Band-Aids. Shouldn't a doctor be able to cure himself of something like that?

"What didn't he pay attention to?" I said.

She thought about this for a moment. "Well," she said, "I've had a bit of a problem and he didn't catch it. I don't want him doing the same thing with you."

She didn't mention the word "cancer," and she didn't explain what Dr. Jaron had done and not done about her "bit of a problem." I suspect—now, not then—that he'd been slow to act when she found the lump, and then had been too laconic when the biopsy proved the lump malignant, treating it as if it was her problem and not his. Many years later she told me, out of the blue, that he hadn't caught it because he didn't like to touch women's breasts.

No doubt his casualness after the fact had something to do with covering his ass, as doctors do, then and now, by acting as if everything is routine, what's the hurry? Yet it might have been more simple. My mother may have decided that Dr. Jaron either lacked sufficient expertise, or interest—who could trust breast examinations to a doctor who didn't like to touch breasts? So, she took matters into her own hands. When she did that, how could she continue to send her children to him?

Or maybe I just didn't ask any questions. A new doctor? One without skin rashes? Why not?

The other datum I have is more flimsy still. When she announced that "Larry" Maxwell was her new doctor, she made a point of saying that he was a man that she trusted. I may have thought about asking why—simple curiosity. But more likely, I deduced that she'd gone to Larry Maxwell because he was a family friend with whom she and my father often socialized. I didn't think to ask why I was now going to a *third* doctor, which would have forced her to explain what was really going on. When she announced that she was going to Vancouver for a trip, I didn't ask why, either.

I was, in other words, oblivious to the most catastrophic event in my mother's entire life while it was happening. My obliviousness didn't end there, either. I remained woefully ignorant about dates, times, effects of the mastectomy and the several courses of radiation treatments she suffered through over the next several years. Worse, I was utterly without empathy about the pain and suffering she experienced. For instance, I believed that the diagnosis had come in 1958, when I was 14—thus partly excusing my indifference on the grounds of my youth. But it turns out I was 16, and the 3-year crisis from diagnosis through surgery to radiation treatment took me past the age of 18—making me a self-involved near-adult instead of an oblivious adolescent.

I have just three other memories of it to work with, and all three of them are brief and mainly about me.

The first is a vague recollection of my mother coming off the plane from Vancouver with her left arm in a sling. I'd gone out to the small airport in Prince George along with my father and sister Nina—my sister Serena was already married and living in Kamloops, 500 kilometres south, and god only knows where my brother was that day—did my father have him stay behind to deal with some delivery that needed to be made? I remember this event more because of the novelty of going to the airport than any sense of dire occasion. As she descended, very uncertainly, the steel staircase from the plane onto the tarmac, she had, I recall, her light-coloured coat half on, her right arm in the coat sleeve, the left sleeve draped over the sling that immobilized her left arm, obscuring it. I remember being surprised at the sling, and I have to imagine, now, that she was pale. Did she smile when she saw us?

What happened after we picked her up is a total blank. It is blank about the remainder of that day, and blank for months and even years after that. Now that I think of it, I have very few tactile memories of any kind from this period of my life, except for sideswiping a telephone pole with the new-from-the-Europe-trip Volkswagen when my father forced a driving lesson on me as a sixteenth-birthday present.

The driving lesson hadn't felt like much of a birthday present even before I sideswiped the pole and had to sit through what seemed like the 650th lecture about what a boob I was. I knew my father only wanted me to get my licence so I could drive delivery vans and trucks for him. I had no objection to that, but no burning interest, either. The important thing, in my mind, was that I had no choice. I was correct about not having a choice. Three days later I took my driving test on a 1956 3-ton Chevrolet flat-deck painted Orange Crush colours. The truck, mercifully for me and for the safety of others, had been unloaded for the test. I passed, but I was a lousy driver. I had four small accidents over the next two months before I smartened up and recognized that I had to actually drive the car *all the time* while I was behind the wheel. In one of the accidents, I drove the Volkswagen through a supermarket window after my foot slipped off the brake pedal and hit the gas as I zipped through the supermarket's parking lot. Bwam! The others were lapses of attention: I'd decided it was more interesting to do or think about other things. Bwam!

The second memory is wholly fabricated, because I was only *told* it happened, years later, and it subsequently burned into my brain as an event I'd witnessed. The night before she flew to Vancouver for the mastectomy (Did I go the airport to see her off? Did I try to reassure her before she left?) my father sat her down at the kitchen table and had her sign a dozen blank cheques.

I understood what this was about the instant I was told about it. I was in my twenties at the time, and when I asked, rhetorically, why my father would do such a thing, my mother rolled her eyes and said, "Guess."

Nah, there was no guessing needed. He'd wanted to be able to clean out her private bank account and the several joint accounts in case . . . Well, I'm sure you get it. It was a horrible thing to do, and it was wholly in character. A sensible woman today would leave a marriage over such a stunt. My mother, a deeply sensible woman, didn't, and not just, I think, because it was a different era.

The third memory is tactile, and not quite so spare. Several months after she returned home from the operation, she called me into her bedroom.

"It's time you had a look at this," she said, her voice matter-of-fact. I was standing just inside the bedroom door as she slipped her nightgown from her left shoulder to expose the vast plate of scar tissue for me to view. I was horrified, by its extent and by the incontrovertible injury of it. Not only was the breast gone, but there was a cavity in her upper chest where the doctors had removed the lymph glands from her left armpit, taking with it elements of her shoulder musculature. The scars were still red and raw-looking, the remaining muscle tissue twisted and cobbled with keloid. (Twenty years later—the next time I had a close look—the scars had changed little.)

"Come here so you can touch it," she ordered.

I sat on the bed beside her, and I remember caressing her cheek—good for me!—before I ran my hand over the scars. The muscles in my groin contracted as I did, as they do to this day when

I recall that moment. Probably, I asked her shyly if it still hurt, and probably, she said "no," or, "not anymore," or, "only sometimes." But maybe I didn't ask.

What I should have recognized, and didn't, was how unnecessarily searing an experience it had been for her, both physically and emotionally, and how tough and decisive she'd been through it. My father, never much help when anyone was in physical pain or discomfort, withdrew from her with cruel swiftness the moment he found out about it.

At the end of that conversation with my sister Nina I had to have so I could pinpoint the dates, Nina recalled two extra details. She had a vivid memory of my mother looking frightened as she boarded the plane to Vancouver. The other was much darker. Dr. Jaron, when he got the results of the biopsy, had phoned my father, not my mother. He phoned on Saturday morning, but it was late Sunday afternoon before my father could work up the nerve to reveal what he'd been told. Fifteen minutes later, he left and went down to the plant. He didn't return home until after ten in the evening. The phone conversation I recorded at the beginning of this took place the next day, and Dr. Jaron had left it to the end of the day to return the call my mother would have made that morning.

My father stayed clear of her for the duration. After the cruelty of the cheques-signings, he delivered her to the plane when she flew to Vancouver for the operation, bringing my sister to the airport to deflect any sharp emotions. He didn't accompany my mother to Vancouver, excusing himself, no doubt, because his business needed him, and anyway, she'd be in good hands down there, right?

She'd had to arrange her treatment by herself, and now she would see it through on her own: the operation, and then the several further trips south for the radiation treatment that were then customary. I try to imagine what she felt when she arrived at the airport in Vancouver that first time, see her hire a taxi to go to the hotel she'd booked, and I try to imagine what went through her mind as she walked into the hospital with her suitcase, and approached the information desk in the hospital lobby to announce who she was, and what she was there to have done to her.

The follow-up radiation treatments likewise, a process that leaves people poisoned and exhausted for weeks afterward: the same flights on the plane alone, the same terrified entry into the hospital lobby. Each time she must have imagined what should have happened: a car ride across town with her husband holding her hand and her children to care for her while she convalesced.

In the fall of 1962, I took off to Europe with a one-way boat ticket in my pocket and $300 in American Express traveller's cheques. My urge to get out of town had acted like a giant slingshot, and it sent me 9500 kilometres before I felt the slightest tug in the other direction. I might not have felt any tug at all, but I was in mid-Atlantic when the Cuban Missile Crisis peaked, and it scared the hell out of me. My travelling companions and I spent most of the crisis in the ship's radio room, watching the captain agonize about whether he ought to turn the ship toward the south Atlantic. I spent several days in that radio room thinking about all the things I was going to miss if the Russians and the Americans blew up the world, and somewhere in the top ten, but not in the top five, was my mother.

When I arrived in London, there was a letter from her worrying that I was okay. I answered the letter, but I wrote just one more letter to her in the next eight months, even though I had to be bailed out of money trouble twice, once by my father and the second time, on the sly, by her. No doubt I missed one of her radiation treatments, and yeah, yeah, kids are always self-centred.

When I returned from Europe, my always-uneasy relationship with my father bloomed into open hostility. Since he'd rescued me when I was in Europe, in his mind that meant that I owed him. He announced that I'd had my fun, and now it was time for me to get serious: come to work for him, get on with my life as a business-man, his assistant CEO, like my older brother.

If I was ever tempted by that, I don't remember it. But I was tempted by other things—money, cars, the usual things that come with money. When I decided that I needed a car, my mother stepped in.

"No," she said. "You don't want a car. If you need one, you can use mine. Owning a car will trap you, and soon you'll be working for your father, and all those plans you have for your life will go up in smoke. And you don't have to pay your father back. I will, if it comes to that. You go out and do something with that brain of yours. Be yourself."

I did exactly what she said, and the battles with my father esca-lated, occasionally into physical confrontations. As the fights grew more intense, my mother interceded more frequently, and more openly on my side, even when I was just being a jerk. I had no clear idea how I was supposed to "be myself," but I learned that if I got in my father's face, I was able to improvise, and the results were dra-matic. So when he said yes, I said no. If he said the sky was blue, I countered that it was green, or grey, or black. If I didn't know who I was, at least I discovered that it was something to not be him, and the more I wasn't him, the more exhilarating life became.

My mother let me know, never quite directly, that she approved, and I was having too much fun to think about her motives. At one level, I trusted her, so she must have had good reasons. At another, our clandestine alliance served my half-cooked agenda, and I wasn't so dumb that I didn't see that it served some needs she had. When she argued with my father, it usually took the heat off me, at least until the next confrontation. Their arguments escalated, as mine did with my father, although theirs never quite got to physical violence. Some of the arguments centred around me, but not all, and maybe not even most. They were at war and I'd chosen my side in it.

*   *   *

There is injury in life, and then there is harm. They're different, and the distinction is important. The injury my mother suffered from the mastectomy was real and substantial. It was a *radical* mastectomy, of a kind not much perpetrated anymore, a vicious intrusion into a woman's body that is both physically traumatic and permanently disfiguring. But it was an injury that successfully healed and because it permitted her to survive another 40 years, she accepted it.

Rita Surry, which is who she had to become in those three years, not the Rita Fawcett she'd grown used to being, or, still more tertiarily, my mother, was a robust woman, and she learned to live with all the physical consequences of what was done to save her life, even finding it a source of entertainment. Reconstructive surgery wasn't really an option then, and I'm not sure she'd have availed herself of it had it been. Careful as she was about her appearance and grooming, she was not a vain person, and she didn't for a moment want to accept that she was a victim, or remain one. She showed me the prosthetic breast that provided the appearance of physical symmetry. She referred to it, always with a laugh, as her "fake boob." For laughs—although not in public—she sometimes would pull it out and throw it at family members. She threw it into my first wife's lap the first time I brought her home for Christmas, in order, she explained, "to make her feel part of the family."

But the *harm* done to her by cancer and its cure was another matter, and I think she sustained more harm than anyone understood, particularly when it came to her relationship with my father.

Yes, she survived. So did the marriage, sort of. She survived in no small part because she was as robust emotionally as she was physically, and because in this situation, and through most of her life, she was utterly, coldly competent whenever the shit hit the fan.

"You do what you have to when there's trouble," she told me one time when she was in her seventies and I was mired in one of my domestic catastrophes. "You deal with the trouble in front of you, and then you can indulge your feelings. You do it in this order because there are kids depending on you, and because you have to take care of them no matter what you're feeling. You can deal with your feelings later, when you have time. They're a luxury, and they don't help anyone, including you. They're real enough, but they're not what moves the mountains."

She said this without bravado, and over the years I'd seen her practise it often enough that I accepted it—and more important—tried to do the same thing myself, sometimes successfully. My father, for all his ambition and foresight, offered nothing I wanted to emulate. He might have been tough on the street or at his business desk, but he was a man who vanished whenever domestic life got rough. If he responded, it was usually to lose his temper, and when that happened, it was time to get under the nearest table. He was always ready to talk *at* us, but he wasn't comfortable with the give-and-take of conversation, not with anyone. If it wasn't about him or his ideas or his products, he just wasn't very interested. If it was about you, well, he could offer himself as a model, or give advice or lend you money, generally with so many strings attached to it that it didn't feel like generosity or help. Then he'd order you to do things his way if you didn't want him thinking you were an idiot. He couldn't collaborate with anyone unless there was advantage to him, and even then, it had to be him in control, front and centre.

These are, I now realize, fairly exact enumerations of my mother's chronic complaints about him, and the primary source of the loneliness that troubled her. The loneliness made her miserable, but she wasn't destroyed by it. Misery and happiness can and do coexist, and for the years of that crisis, she had a lot to live for: four children, three young grandchildren, a community of people she liked, and a landscape she loved. And so the misery and pain inflicted on her coexisted with the small, intense moments of happiness you could always read in her as near-equal tributaries of her life, like the Nechako and Fraser rivers that met at Prince George. The Nechako in those days was blue and sparkling, the Fraser muddy and fouled with upstream debris from the wild MacGregor River basin, the distant Rockies, and too much careless logging.

I suppose most people's lives are like those conjoining rivers— a composite of sweet and nasty, experience and aspiration, currents that nurture; shoals and back eddies that diminish and corrode. Or they would be, if human life was something that could be accurately judged in the abstract: overflown in plan view, say, or rendered coherent by the exquisition of physical details and symbolic dialogue, the way flowery novelists do it. Those gods we invent to explain life's arbitrariness and misery likewise tempt me here, because the hand of God can excuse any transgression.

But this is a real life, lived by a real river, and this is a real woman in real pain. These are components of human happiness, such as it is.

Some Stories about Roast Beef

ARTLEY FAWCETT was a lifelong connoisseur of roast beef. He'd been a salesman for a meat-packing company after all, and he knew his cuts: shell bone for an oven roast, baron of beef for barbecuing, always on a rotisserie, and don't put any Smarties on it: beef should taste like beef, not like some garlicked-up stew, and not slathered with crap that makes it taste like it escaped from a delicatessen. I don't think I ever saw him actually put anything in the oven—the kitchen, as I've noted, belonged solely to my mother while she was alive—but he critiqued every roast she cooked, and without mercy. When he cranked up the barbecue, it was bugger off and don't offer advice.

We ate a lot of roast beef, and there was just one way for it to arrive on the table: rare. Not medium rare, not blue, but rare. If the serving platter wasn't at least a centimetre deep in juices by the time he'd carved a half-dozen slices from it, there was an uproar and it wasn't just my father making the critique. We all preferred beef the same way, and at the close of dinner there was a 30-second period of grace where table manners were suspended so we could spoon the platter clear—now 2 centimetres deep in juices. That concluded, English table manners were reinstated and we sedately ate our desserts as if we were civilized people.

While I was a kid, corporate executives from the companies from whom my father held franchises—Orange Crush, Pepsi-Cola, and Canada Dry—periodically showed up to cavort with the country yokels, and, I suppose, to make sure we were upholding the corporations' standards. If they happened to be in town over the weekend, these men would be invited to Sunday Roast Beef Dinner.

My mother cooked these roasts, but it was my father who carved them. He owned a carving knife with a 25-centimetre blade that he honed so finely that it was sharp enough to shave with. He used it to carve carpaccio-thin slices from the roast. Then, deploying the deep notch at the tip of the blade, he'd serve these thin slices by flicking them, Frisbee style, across the dinner table so that they landed on the guests' plates, splat! Depending on how stuffed the shirts of these out-of-town guests were, he would warn them of what he was about to do—or not. He never missed his target, and I'm not exactly referring to whether the slices of beef landed on the right dinner plate, which they nearly always did. My mother, who officially disapproved of this practice but occasionally cracked a small smile when he did it, then passed the Yorkshire pudding, which was *her* specialty, and asked the guests how they were enjoying northern British Columbia.

Few of these men asked for second helpings. If they did, they received it the same way, and though they seldom understood it, they'd passed a test of character that my father took more than just a little seriously. He didn't respect men he could intimidate.

At the last Family Reunion my father attended, and the first one at which he had not personally executed the barbecuing of the baron of beef, we also held a shareholders' meeting for the family company so we'd all be able to write off the expense of getting there. My father was 98 at the time, and had given up control of the company several years before, so his presence at the meeting was largely ceremonial—or would have been had he not been who and what he was.

My brother gave a short recitation of the company acquisitions and expenses for the year just passed, blah, blah, then brought in his accountant to explain the fine details, blah, blah. My father listened to everything said, but asked no questions. In fact, he seemed vaguely bored, an uncharacteristic response that had me suspecting he was up to something. As the meeting wound down, my brother, looking as wary as I was feeling, paused ostentatiously, and asked my father if he had anything he wanted to say. My father said nothing for a moment, almost as if he hadn't heard the question. But then he gathered himself in his chair, reflected for a longer interval, and said, yes, as a matter of fact, he did have something to say. But first, he wanted a glass of water. Several of us moved to get it for him, but no, he'd get it himself.

He got to his feet, shook himself like a retriever exiting a lake with a duck in its mouth, and disappeared into the house, leaving us to stew over what he was about to do to us. Each of us assumed we were in for a tongue-lashing, but about exactly what, we had no clue. I thought it was going to be about the modest directors' fees the company paid us, which my brother had seen fit to increase. My brother shrugged when I asked if he thought that was what we were going to get it for, saying that my father already knew about the increase, and appeared not to mind. "It's something else," he said.

My father was gone several long minutes, and when he returned, there was no glass of water in his hand. He sat down at the head of the table, genuflected for a moment, then sat up in his chair and looked each of us in the eye, one after another.

"I didn't like the beef this year," he said, and launched into a detailed critique of how it had been dry, overcooked, and tasteless. My brother tried to explain that his wife's family preferred their beef well-done, but my father wasn't having any of *that*, and by this point, I'd changed sides. The beef *hadn't* been very good, and my father was completely right.

We sat through the diatribe, stunned but relieved. He was almost through before I caught the slight grin tugging at the corners of his mouth. He never again talked about business to any of us except my brother. But he wanted us to know he hadn't lost his stuff.

August 1966

H ARTLEY FAWCETT had a fruitful relationship with Lady Luck. His most serious scrape, in 1947, involved the car he was driving and a bull moose. The car was totalled and the moose died, but he walked away with nothing more than a few bruises and a good story to tell his customers.

It wasn't that he was manic about risk avoidance, either. He just didn't volunteer himself or his money when the odds were against him, and he possessed a mental and physical agility that was as much instinctual as learned. He was a frugal man, he worked hard without ever putting his head down or cutting corners, and he never made a show of whatever cards he held. When he saw an opportunity, he thought it through and if he decided it was a good one, he lunged, with coordination and absolute concentration.

He was also physically tough, and as I've noted, he had the courage of a man with strong convictions. He didn't start fights unless it was with Ron and me and when he was in one he kept his wits about him, counterpunched, and when he did, he hit as hard as he could.

When I was 11 years old I was with him when a logger in a pickup truck rear-ended us. My father asked me if I was okay, then got out of the car, looked at the slight damage to his car, and shrugged. From inside the car, I watched the logger stagger out of his truck and lurch toward my father, who pointed to the back of our car and said something, probably about the logger's lousy driving skills or his state of sobriety. The logger, a man at least 10 centimetres taller, instantly launched a haymaker. My father easily dodged the punch, and as the logger wound up for another, my father hit him with two short punches, a right and a left, bang, bang. The logger went sprawling, unconscious, across the sidewalk.

My father got back into the car, muttered "stupid bastard," and drove off. He was scowling, but he wasn't even breathing hard. I don't think he was cursing out the logger as much as he was criticizing his dumb tactics.

Lucky? I guess so. But steely nerves and an ability to think on your feet have ways of creating luck, and so does a dislike of losing. My father was cool under fire, and his hatred of losing was passionate, whether it was an argument, a fist fight, a customer account gone delinquent, or a long-term contest of will. He found ways to win what he could, but he wasn't a fool, either. He'd vacate the field if he saw the odds were against him.

If you'd asked him what his worst defeat was, he'd tell you that it was the way he retired from business. That's a complicated story that didn't involve luck in the smallest way. It was something that started a long way from who and what he was, but it ended up as close to his hard heart as anything ever got.

In the early 1960s, the big manufacturing and consumer corporations began to descend on northern British Columbia, targeting the local businesses that had been operating for years and were now becoming prosperous. Businesses like his.

It had begun in the lumber industry, kicked off by the government's announcement that pulp mills were on the way, and that forest tenure, which until then was held on a near-hereditary basis, would be taken to competitive bidding. Few saw this as anything less than a positive development: more competition meant more profits, more jobs, a spur to population growth—the standard bullshit slung by business boosters and the Chamber of Commerce.

But competition for the seemingly limitless supply of timber quickly turned vicious, touching off a melee amongst the local mill owners trying to sequester the best stands of timber for the cutting of structure wood—the 2 x 4–inch studs universally used for building that had long been the local industrial bread and butter—or to sell it off to the pulp mills when they arrived. And so the multinationals came, companies that wanted the wood for the spaghetti-mills they would build, or pulp fibre, or log exports: whatever else sweetened their bottom line.

In 1956, there were 600 mills in the area, all independently owned and operated, many of them one- to four-man gypo mills portable enough to be moved from cut block to cut block. The 50 or 60 larger mills pretty much held proprietary rights to whichever area they'd located in, and with the generally held belief that the forests would last forever, they'd done little to protect their tenure and less to protect the health of the forests or perpetuate the supply of trees.

Now they found themselves having to make bids on each timber block the Forest Service partitioned for cutting, and there was, at first, not a little poaching going on between the more aggressive locals. Once the poaching took hold, the multinationals moved in, licking their chops like coyotes that had discovered an unguarded bunny hutch. They'd been the ones who'd bullied the government into the timber-rights bidding system, using the public argument that it would improve government revenues—and deploying the equally alluring backroom argument that it was good capitalism and, no doubt hinting that it would result in generous campaign donations. By the time the smoke cleared in 1972, all but a few of the gypos were gone, 8 supermills had replaced the 60 bigger independents, and there were 2 pulp mills stinking up the town and spewing chemicals into the rivers. Only one of this whole bunch was locally owned.

Something similar happened within the city limits. A&W was the first consumer franchise to arrive, followed soon after by Dairy Queen, McDonald's, and a raft of others. The local eateries soon began to falter and die off. The same currents moved through the entire local economy: owners replaced by branch managers, and the profits vacuumed out of town to Vancouver and beyond.

I don't think my father saw the axe head heading his way, too. He'd held his Orange Crush, Pepsi, and Canada Dry soft drink franchises for years, and the franchisers were more than happy with his market shares. When his competition in the ice cream business, owned by a Vancouver-based lumber baron who'd already lost most of his timber-cutting rights along with the rest of the locals, was bought out by a big Alberta-based dairy company, my father sneered that it was just rich outsiders buying out other rich outsiders, and that if he could beat the old one he could beat the new ones—although he did hedge his bet by running ads on the local radio station about the virtues of supporting local industry. He still had plenty of fire in his belly, and he had two sons coming up behind him to take over. What could go wrong?

One fall afternoon in 1965, a couple of business-suited executives from the biggest dairy consortium in B.C.'s lower mainland walked into his office and announced that if he didn't sell his ice cream operation to them, they'd dump product into his marketplace below his cost until he was bankrupt.

He threw them out. But two weeks later, he got a letter from the B.C. Milk Board informing him that using the best raw milk supply in the area for something as non-essential as ice cream was a violation of board policy and Not in the Public Interest, and my father found himself faced with the prospect of making his ice cream, of which he was justly proud, from more costly and inferior powdered-milk stock and coconut oil.

He reconsidered—or as he put it, Faced Up to Reality. "You Can't Fight Progress," he said, spinning the bad news into the core of his philosophy for everything else. "This is all Predestined: the Big Fish eat the Small Fish. Capitalism is no different from the Forces of Nature."

He took the dairy consortium's offer, and was out of the business inside six months. But he'd been running two businesses in the same operation, and his soft drink operation, less complicated logistically and more lucrative, was expanding. He'd recently acquired the franchise for 7Up, and now had four of the five most popular brands coming off his trucks—and he held a loan chit on the local Coca-Cola bottler, who was a former employee he'd bankrolled when the hapless previous owner gave up and wanted out.

My father was closing in on his 60th birthday, and he'd been on a 15-year winning streak. He assumed that with two grown sons

working under him, he could start another, greater streak. What he didn't see coming at him was a piece of biology.

My father, you see, was the purest strain of alpha male, and that meant he wasn't capable of allowing any other dog around him with its tail up, not even for a moment. The problem was that Ron and I had bred true: each of us born with a bushy tail that naturally stood straight up even though we were fundamentally different from one another. Ron had gladly worked for my father since he was 14 or 15 years old, was quick to learn from him, eager to follow his footsteps and habits, most eager of all to gain his acceptance and praise—provided that it involved respect that could be earned by hard work, and some autonomy.

I was five years younger, more willful but with less aptitude and poorer focus. But I was much more curious about the world beyond my father's business, and completely cantankerous whenever anyone tried to put a thumb on me. I liked the work well enough, but in high school I was more often truant at the after-school jobs he set up for me than I was for my school classes.

The job I liked the best was typing his business letters, which, until I arrived, were being typed by a secretary whose native language was Dutch. She typed the letters exactly as he wrote them, which was a problem because my father used a punctuation system all his own: he capitalized any word that he thought was important, and rarely used periods, commas, or question marks. My father wrote a lot of letters, some the predictable ones to customers demanding payment, but others to his distributors and franchisers, sometimes to complain about something specific, but more often to explain why he was right about everything under the sun, and they weren't. The more philosophical he waxed, the longer the letters got, and the more capital letters he used. By the time I was in Grade 10, I'd decided that he was making a fool of himself, and pretty much took over as his personal typist. His secretary was happy to let me type the letters, since she had no idea what he was saying and was a peck-and-poke typist who found his wordiness heavy going. My father didn't seem to mind me typing them until I started deleting his ideas and adding ideas of my own, most of which launched from pretty well the opposite of what he had in mind. After that, I'd find some of the letters I'd been fiddling with waiting for me in the basket when I arrived after school, with my stuff crossed out and even more capitalized words scribbled in the margins than I'd replaced. A couple of times he lost his temper and demanded that I type exactly what he'd written. I'd tone it down for a week or two, then start messing around again. Through high school, it was the one forum in which we could argue and I had the advantage.

When my brother finished high school he bought a car and went to work for my father, ready to work his way up what he knew would be a very short ladder. I spent the year after I graduated in Europe, and when I got home, my father expected I'd do the same. He'd bailed me out of the trouble I got into overseas, remember, and in his mind, my wild oats were sown, I owed him, and it was time to pony up.

Instead, I joined the Forest Service after one of our scraps, then worked in a local menswear store and lived in a two-room shack across town that had no running water or toilet but was a fine place to party and stay up all night. The shack had been provided for me rent free by one of my father's many enemies, all of whom seemed to find me pretty entertaining. And why wouldn't they? I was a weird kid who enjoyed reading, wanted an education, and planned to write books of his own. But I was my mother's son, too, so I also kept coming back home regularly, and my father kept baiting the hook, not always patiently and almost never cheerfully, for me to settle down and do what my brother had done.

I worked for him on and off, enjoying the physical labour and the camaraderie with his employees even though I wasn't particularly good with the trucks or the business side of it, and bemused that my father didn't seem to notice. But my tail kept springing to high alert around him, and this was something he always noticed. We had one dust-up after another, and whenever we did, I walked away and did something else, enjoying it most when I could see it pissed him off.

I took off to university in January 1966, the first in the family to do this, but when I came home that summer, I again worked on the trucks for him. Oblivious as ever, I barely noticed his agitation at losing the ice cream side of the business. He'd made my brother his sales supervisor, and Ron made it part of his duties to stay between my father and me. Ron was, I think, trying to protect me, although that, like the rest, I barely registered. I worked long hours, got paid generously, banked every cent of it, and made plans for all the things I was going to do when I returned to the coast in September.

Ten days before I was to return to Vancouver for my second semester of university, my father called Ron and me into his office. I sat down, wondering what I'd screwed up, and idly stoked my testosterone for the coming fight. But my father had an odd gleam in his eye, and he didn't seem, as he normally was, angry or even exasperated with me. I sprawled into the inside chair, and as I did, registered the tactical datum that if things got nasty, I'd have to crawl over Ron to get out.

"Oh, damn," I said. "I need a Pepsi. Let me out, eh?"

I clambered across Ron's lap, found a half-full case beside the rear entrance to the general office, picked up two bottles and used one to crack open the second. I took a couple of glugs, in no hurry to return to what I expected would turn out to be another lecture about my incompetence or my father's upper case Business Philosophy.

"Shove over," I said to Ron when I returned. He gave me a barely raised eyebrow, and moved to the inner chair. I sat down and looked at my father. He was sitting upright behind his desk with his hands folded together, smiling mirthlessly at our exchange. He tapped his right index finger on a sheaf of foolscap in front of him, and cleared his throat. Now what?

"I want," he said, in his best capital-letter voice, "to present to you my Grand Plan For The Future."

I glanced across at Ron. He was staring intently at my father as if this were a long-expected moment.

"Whose future?" I asked, chancing a quick argument in the hope it might change the tone, which already felt oppressive.

"Your Future," my father said. He turned his gaze to Ron. "And yours. And mine. Most of all, the Future of This Company, and all the Thousands of Dollars it can put in Your Pockets."

He swept his hands wide. "Not to mention the Joys of Accomplishment."

I turned in my chair so I could gauge how Ron was taking this. He was still staring at my father, but now I detected a wariness. I cleared my throat, hoping it would control the nervous giggle I could feel rising in the pit of my stomach.

"I have the Grand Plan, all of it, Up Here." He pointed to his head with one finger. "I've been thinking this over for six months. We have to Move Ahead, and here's how I propose to do it. Ron, you're going to Take Over at Grande Prairie."

Two years ago, my father had bought out another bottler in northern Alberta, built a new building, added a couple of franchises so that the product list was identical to the operation in Prince George, improved the production equipment, and moved his best driver-salesman up to run it.

"You," he said, nodding his head at me, "will Take Over here. Under my Guidance, naturally."

Then, as if he was stuck for something philosophical with which to seal the deal, he said, "The Future is Limitless. All We Have to Do is Work Together."

The small office slowly filled with a poisonous silence. What I'd heard was that I'd been chosen over my brother to run the big operation. Since I was going back to university, this was stupid as well as unfair. Ron was being sent away from my father, the only place he'd ever wanted to be. And being under my father's thumb was the *last* place I wanted to be. How could he have gotten this so wrong?

In Ron's eyes, I saw hurt and then something that looked like anger. My father stared at each of us in turn for a longer-than-comfortable moment, clearly bewildered by our less-than-enthusiastic response.

"Listen," he said to me. "I'll have you Sitting on a Sandy Beach in Hawaii with a Redhead by the time you're thirty. You'll be a Millionaire."

"I don't want to go to Hawaii," I said, without thinking. "And I don't like redheads." The part of my brain that was cowed and confused was thinking, "He doesn't know who you are or what you want." But the larger part, the one that was sucking up the endorphins of outrage, won out.

"No," I said, as much to myself as to him. "This isn't fair to Ron. He should run this operation, whether or not I go back to university. And I'm going back there in September whether you like it or not."

My brother cleared his voice. "I don't like this either," he said, quietly. "What happens to Gerry?"

Gerry was the current manager, and Ron's close friend.

"We'll have to let Gerry go," my father said, beginning to flush with displeasure. "I've decided that he Doesn't Have What It Takes. And Now's the Time to Move Forward."

"No," Ron said. His voice had a flat resolve I hadn't heard before, ever.

I could see my father trying to compose himself. There was something in his eyes I hadn't seen before, something that wasn't the anger I was expecting. Fear? No, not that, but akin to it. Anger I could deal with, because that's what I was used to. I was as afraid of him as I'd always been, but I forced myself to go into the automatic pilot I'd learned, confronting his anger with aggression and letting the two spin into yelling and threats. This would permit me to walk away, as I had before, secure in the knowledge that my mother would intercede, pull me back in.

"I'm going back to university," I said, and got to my feet.

My father did the same, but we didn't make eye contact. Ron stayed in his chair. He didn't look any happier than my father did. "You boys Think About What I've Said, and Give Me Your Thoughts," he said. I was halfway down the hall when he added, in distinctly lower case tones, "These are just proposals, you know."

*   *   *

I went back to Vancouver ten days later to start my university classes. I didn't give my father my thoughts before I left. The truth was that I didn't have any particular thoughts about his Grand Plan, and I was pretty sure he wasn't interested in my thoughts about The Plan or about anything else even if I'd had them. Two months after that, Ron walked into his office and told him he was quitting. He moved to Kamloops, got a job there, and tried to get on with his life. A month after that, my father started negotiations to sell the business. Within a year he'd moved himself and my mother to the Okanagan Valley, and was living on the shores of Skaha Lake, retired.

I didn't talk to my father about his Grand Plan for almost 20 years. When I did, we were in his big Cadillac, driving to Edmonton on the one road trip we ever made together. I think I was trying to offer a backhanded apology for hurting him all those years ago, but it came out wrong. I asked him what he'd been thinking when he wanted to put me in charge of the big operation and send my brother away.

"I was trying to give you a world," he said, without looking at me. "But you thought you knew everything, and you didn't want it."

"I wanted my own world," I said, and left it at that. Another 17 years went by before the subject hit the table again. When it did, I heard the same bitter anger and disappointment in his voice: I'd thrown away his world.

And this could be the end of it, another story of miscommunication between fathers and true-bred sons. I could accuse him of not being able to bear having his sons around him with their bushy tails up, of not seeing our need for autonomy, of not letting us live on our own terms. And that would all be true. But it isn't the whole story. There are two more parts to this story, and they're quite different.

One is about my brother. My father, you see, hoped Ron would come back, and he waited very patiently. And slowly, gradually, my brother came back. It wasn't easy for either of them, and it didn't always go well, but eventually, they rebuilt the Grand Plan so that it was *their* plan. Given that every independent soft drink bottler in British Columbia was gone by 1980—absorbed by the corporations—their Revised Grand Plan is almost certainly better and grander than the original could have turned out. It's also better because in the Revised Grand Plan, Ron's two sons work for him, and as far as I can see, with their tails straight up.

The other chapter is mine, and it is an after-the-fact admission of debt. I did go back to university that fall, just as I intended, and I did it without regrets and without looking back. I made a very different life than the one my father tried to plan for me: no Hawaii, no Redheads on a Sandy Beach. My father never quite understood why I did the things I did, and I'd be kidding myself if I said I thought he believed that what I pursued in life was worthwhile: "Book-learned nonsense," he'd grumble, "not worth the powder to blow it to hell."

But—and this is what matters—he went along with it anyway, and he sent me money so I could stay at university without very much hardship. He was grudging and ungracious about it, and he always tried to attach strings. But now I see that he ignored it when I snipped the strings, and he didn't really demand that I be directly grateful for his help. I don't know if he was proud of the books I've written. But I do know he read them all, and occasionally, he'd correct errors of fact I'd made, nearly always with an "aha!" that made the windows vibrate.

I owe him for all of it, and it's my shame that this half-assed posthumous acknowledgment is the only one he ever got.

A Photo Album, with Commentary

---

*J*UST AFTER my father's death in 2008, my brother, Ron, digitized roughly 500 of my parents' colour slides taken in the 1950s and 1960s, and sent them to each family member on a pair of DVDs. I copied the DVDs into the picture folders in both of my computers, one of which, the laptop, regularly sits on the counter that separates the kitchen of my house from the dining room.

The slides Ron digitized had been languishing in my parents' basement for 40 years, relics of bypassed technology and social habits—in this case, the interminable slide shows that most children in that era had to suffer through after family trips and holiday seasons. Most of the pictures I'd seen many times before, but always socially and without leisure, projected on a fold-up screen with the pacing determined by someone else's agenda, usually—okay, always—my father's.

Ron had digitized just 500 out of the 2000 or so slides in the basement, and for a good reason. The other 1500 were scenery, which the introduction and wide distribution in the early 1950s of 35-millimetre colour film and improved lenses made more attractive to photograph. That's also why many of the 500 slides that made my brother's cut feature family members photographed off in the distance, tiny foreground authenticants to the scenery my father loved. Nearly all the slide shows I was subjected to as a kid were narratives about where and how my parents holidayed, which is to say, look at all those bloody trailers parked by that lake and how much do you think they cost? Or how about those mountains in the distance shimmering with light, and gee, look at that bank of cloud hanging over that lake, is that a rainbow?

I was interested, then as now, in people. When I look at a photograph, I want to know what's going on in people's minds, posed or unguarded. During my father's slide shows, I peppered him with questions about who they travelled with or who they met when they got to their destination, and what they talked about, what they were like—until I was told to shut up. Some dopey geographical detail 20 miles in the distance that we'd never get close to, and which would probably be logged or burned within a decade, interested me not in the least, particularly when it was my old man supplying the narrative and my fellow British Columbians administering the destruction.

So really, it wasn't the slides shows I hated all those years ago, it was scenery. My father loved scenery. Once he had the money and the leisure, he perched himself and his homes on the shores of lakes or atop hills with vistas of river valleys so he could view the scenery, spout platitudes about it, and enumerate the development possibilities that would sully its beauty. It saddled me with a lifelong dislike for the far distance. Or maybe it is the onslaught of platitudes that always seems to spout from people's mouths while they're standing in front of a scenic view.

It occurred to me while I was watching these same photographs scrolling digitally across my laptop screen for the first time that I had never before had the luxury of being able to study their contents on any schedule of my own devising. If you sat a colour slide in front of a projector too long, the projection bulb would fry the

image, and so it was move on, move on, and don't dawdle or reflect. Unless my father was photographing some boring vista, that was pretty much his general ethos in those years.

I was able to watch this new slide show because my laptop has a screen saver that chooses photographs at random from the machine's picture folder, and runs them on a more or less endless loop. Thus, almost 50 years after my father's photographs were taken, I can watch a twenty-first-century version of those old slide shows, this time on a much more watchable screen size of 9 x 11 inches, and with a pacing that anyone sitting at the kitchen counter can control simply by manipulating the keyboard's forward and backward arrows.

After watching several hundred always-unique yet utterly connected slide shows on my kitchen laptop, I've discovered something important and ineluctably true about my parents and about my family that I missed utterly while I was in the middle of the story. I missed it, I suppose, because I wanted the narrative to be about me and not family, or maybe I just missed it because I was young and stupidly impatient.

Here's the thing: Hartley Fawcett and Rita Surry, individually and together, based on the only documentary evidence that exists now that they're not around to interfere with their nostalgic and possibly disappointed testimony, were, despite the protracted war they waged against one another, happy and comfortable people, the alpha male and female of several sizable social and economic communities they were part of.

Now I hear the objections: these are photographs, many of them posed, and all of them at least subject to the formalities of self-projection. Sure, that's true. But as my father used to say while he was trying to inflict his Philosophy-O-Life on my unwilling ears, "As a Man Thinketh, So He Is." What he meant by this was that an important fuel for happiness is its conscious projection as well as its conscious pursuit.

So let's turn on the projector and see what the pictures have to say.

ONE

This woman is Rita Joan Fawcett, then Rita Surry. She worked as a cashier in the meat department of the Hudson's Bay store in downtown Edmonton. She was a dance club queen, and girl-about-town. It is 1933, and she is 23 years old, about to meet Duncan Hartley Fawcett, the man she will marry in 1936.

She's a big-boned girl, buxom, pretty without quite being beautiful, but healthy and very well-groomed, always. Those are silk stockings on her legs, the watch on her left wrist will last 40 years, her manicure is impeccable but not ostentatious, and the necklace—are they real pearls?—is tasteful.

Her best asset is her smile, which could still light up rooms when she was 90, and made her friends all her life without making her seem goofy or an easy mark. Behind it was a quick and an encompassing sense of humour that didn't require malice or *schadenfreude* to fire it up, and which masked her native shrewdness. There are no photographs of her in which she looks like a deer in the headlights, and I never saw her in real life that way. Her weakness was that she couldn't see things coming. She only saw people coming, about whom she often made snap judgments that were rarely off the mark—and nearly always final. She kept her feet on the ground her entire life, and taught the skill to her children. This was no small accomplishment, given their very different characters.

TWO

When my father finally moved into a rest home, I found, stashed in the basement of his house, an ancient hard briefcase covered in green alligator skin. It was stuffed with snapshots of himself and what appeared to be the friends he'd had before he met my mother.

I'd never seen any of the snapshots before and I was puzzled by his motives for secreting them away all those years. Was he exercising some strange discretion for my mother's sake, not reminding her that he'd had a life before her? Or were there things in the photographs he did not want included in the family albums—and thus in the family history—for fear his children would discover all the non-Rotarian things he'd done before he got serious and started Thinking and Speaking in Capital Letters? This one made me think it was the latter motive. He's on the left, wearing a patterned sweater and collarless shirt, leaning into a pal who's wearing a vest, tie, and white shirt. Between them is a girl, her hands draped across their shoulders, straddling the two bikes in a pose that doesn't allow us to see which of the two bikes she's on—an important detail?

Probably not, since it's likely another woman took the photograph, and she wasn't my mother either. The bike my father is on is likely his 1927 Indian, which I'd been told about but never seen. It's almost certainly the one he rode across Edmonton's High Level Bridge, down the centre line at 75 mph at noon hour with traffic going both ways, an utterly surprising admission he made to me in 1983 as we passed across the one-way bridge. We were on the way to visit the house in which his family lived for a couple of years before they moved out to Morinville to homestead.

I could never get him to talk about the High Level Bridge incident again. "I was Young and Foolish back then," he'd scoff. "I've seen the Error of my Ways, and made the Necessary Improvements."

What he didn't want us to see, I suspect, is the expressions on his face and his pal's. They're both gazing at the photographer with their mouths slightly twisted into grimaces: tough guys, antediluvian motor-cycle hoodlums, the ancestors of the Hells Angels. But also, young men, free spirits *not* getting on with their lives, not supporters of Rotary or the Chamber of Commerce, not focused on business, business.

At the end of his life, he made some more "necessary improvements," but these ones were in lower case. The most important one was to be less bloody-minded about the young and their foolishness, and about the errors of their ways. But did he buy us all motorcycles, and send us off to get into trouble?

Hell, no.

THREE

The photograph above left, dated the summer before my parents were married in 1936 and discovered after my father's death, caused some discomfort amongst my siblings. Who is the woman? She's not my mother, and she's clearly leaning into my father's hip, while he has his muscled left forearm holding her arm, his stance serious and masculine to the point of *macho*, right down to the second undone button in his short-sleeved shirt. "A hunk," whistled a female friend to whom I showed the photo.

I had the small 2 1/2 x 4 photo, along with several dozen others, digitized, and about a month later, I printed them off in 8 x 11–inch format on my photo printer so I could study them. One of the other photos I printed off was a post-wedding photo of my parents, the one on the right, in which they're standing in a wooded area, my mother leaning into my father with my father's right arm around her waist, more or less cupping her right breast. Both are smiling, my father almost shyly, my mother with a "look-what-I-have" grin on her face. You know the photo is post-wedding because my father has the thin gold wedding band on his left ring finger he wore until he replaced it with a five-carat diamond in 1967, the same year he bought his first Cadillac for my mother to ride in.

It wasn't until I had the extra detail provided by the 8 x 11 that I spotted it: in the mystery photograph, he's wearing his wedding ring. He's also wearing the same shirt in both photographs. The photographer in the mystery photo was almost certainly my mother, and the woman must be her closest friend, Inez Cummings, who's the photographer in the other photo.

FOUR

My parents' generation had to pose for their photographs because the insensitive lenses on their box cameras required it. But they also posed for their pictures because they wanted to memorialize the events and people they lived with and around. They were at the edge of civilization, life was uncertain, and these photographs were the proof that they were in the world. They had to wait weeks while the film was processed and the snapshots printed, and once they had them, they protected them, put them in albums so they could be taken out in some far-off future when it would be hard to remember who they'd been, what they looked like, and where they'd been.

But I think that they sometimes took photographs because they wanted to see if they were beautiful. This young, probably vain young man was photographed at Alberta Beach sometime between 1927 and 1930 while he was in his early twenties. He's good-looking, and he knows it. And so he turns his head to a good angle, smiles, and gazes at the camera as if asking, "What do you say? I'm really something, aren't I?"

He was really something.

FIVE

This is one of my favourite snapshots of my parents together, but I know virtually nothing certain about it: no date, location, occasion, or photographer. Just look at them! She's sitting on his lap, her arm tight around his neck, smiling shyly. That's a fashionable hairstyle, her sweater is elegant, almost as if she's dressed up for the photograph even though they're out in the wilderness.

He's more pensive, gazing at the camera with his head turned at an attractive angle. But his arm is around her waist, so he's there for her, too. I wanted this photograph to be shot upriver from Prince George on the Fraser River, and that would have made it the early 1940s. I wanted it there because it would have been symbolic of their life in northern British Columbia: the two of them alone, making a life in a landscape immensely larger than they are, the river wide and deep, rumbling along as the Fraser does, under the big, empty subarctic sky.

But look more carefully and you'll see that the river behind them is clear, not milky with silt like the Fraser, and nowhere near wide enough. So this is earlier, the river is the North Saskatchewan upriver from Edmonton, and it is the mid-1930s. They are "just" lovers here, at the beginning of their six-decade journey, and they're not even alone because, of course, this was long before cameras were equipped with shutter-delay mechanisms. Who was their witness this time?

The forests across the river were logged long ago, and the water no longer sparkles. The lovers are dead.

SIX

My parents loved the wilderness of British Columbia, its mountains and rivers without end, and whenever they could they travelled to see its scenic landmarks. In this photograph, they're near Kitwanga, just north of Highway 16 off the Cassiar road not far from Hazelton. The year is 1948. They're exploring a salmon-bearing tributary of the Skeena, but neither of them looks very pleased about it. My father has his shoes off, so that explains his expression—the water is cold as hell up there 12 months a year. My mother, hands in pockets like an irritable school-marm, is worrying about how my father is going to get back across the stream without going over the waterfall behind them, or she's hector-ing him, a man who never learned to swim, about not going farther in case he slips and falls in. This, in the midst of such natural beauty.

Did they argue about it in the car all the way to Hazelton? How many such interruptions of happiness did they experience?

Here, for once, you can see exactly what's going through each of their minds:

"What will become of my children if the bloody fool drowns?"

"Will this woman never stop nagging me?"

SEVEN

My father, the gangster. This photograph was taken in the late 1940s, a few years before he left the meat-packing company he'd worked 19 years for so he could buy a rundown soft drink and ice cream manufacturing outfit that eventually will make him a wealthy man.

He's well put together, isn't he? Snap-brim hat, three-piece suit, striped socks long enough that you know he's wearing garters, and the Dack's oxfords he wore every day until he was in his nineties and the company stopped making them. In his left hand he's got his invoice book, a pencil in his right to take more orders, and he's sitting on some of the merchandise he sells. Meat-packing companies didn't just sell meat in those days: there are six cases of canning jars, a case of butter, and at least three cases of Fly-Tox, one of them just behind his right elbow. If you're not sure what *that* is, it was an insect killer that butcher shops in those days sprayed around to keep the flies down, and since it was the late 1940s, it contained DDT.

If people needed something, my father was always the guy to sell it to them. Selling was his chosen method of relating to his fellow humans, and he enjoyed every sales pitch he ever made. He gave up selling DDT to sell ice cream and pop, always without a flicker of second thoughts about socially redeeming activities or the health of the commonwealth. For him, "the customer is always right" covered everything.

It doesn't cover everything in the twenty-first century, but that's our problem, not his.

EIGHT

This is Rita Fawcett as I have her set in my mind today. Not very surprisingly, it is the way she looked in her prime. She's in her early forties here, the year is 1954 or 1955, and she's at work, doing the books for my father's ice cream and soft drink manufacturing plant. This was a job she did during the summers and whenever else my father's leaky accounting skills and heavy-handed treatment of his paid bookkeepers put him in a jam—quite often, in those days. She enjoyed these respites from life as a housewife, and you can see it in her face.

At her best, she was what you see in this photograph: cheerful in public, well-groomed, intelligent, with a finger always on the bottom line. She was also a woman without much native docility, a character trait that preserved both her sanity and her autonomy, and which my father found a never-ending challenge to his masculinity.

But there was more here than a simple contest of wills. However difficult her marriage was, she was a loyal partner to her marriage contract—if not to her husband. Marriage, in her mind, was at once a domestic partnership, and a financial one. In both, she stood her ground without drama and without flinching. If my father screwed up in public, she said nothing until they were alone. Most of the time, anyway.

There were endless arguments between the two of them, but rarely *scenes*, and never physical violence. This in itself was only slightly remarkable, because while my father was a man not averse to violence—he bloodied both my older brother and me several times during our adolescence—he didn't ever direct it toward either my mother or my sisters. Never mind that all three were more insolent to him than my brother or I dared to be.

Was her unapologetic independence the same thing as courage? Perhaps it was. But there was nothing wild in it. For her it was an integral part of the contract between them, and crucial to its strength. She believed it was her job to cover the things he wasn't good at, and she did her job even when it infuriated him. There was a cost attached. Even at this stage of their marriage, both of them respected the contract with more enthusiasm than they did the person they'd made it with.

I liked it when my mother worked. Whenever she was working she was more cheerful at home, and more energetic for months afterward.

And then the winters came.

NINE

My father was a thoughtful man, in several unconventional ways. He was an obsessive thinker, not in the contemplative sense, but in the sheer constancy of his ideation. He had ideas about everything that crossed his path. Some of these ideas were practical, many were philosophical and some were, well, dreadful simplifications or plain wrong. But the best of his ideas were practical, and he often applied them in unorthodox, inspired ways. Had his powers of observation been similarly energetic but more sophisticated than they were, fewer of his ideas would have run aground, and he would have had more second thoughts, of which he had very few, at least in public, until his last decade of life, when he had many surprising ones.

The main reason he was a thoughtful man was that he was interested in everything, and I mean, *every thing*. When he became interested in some physical process, he pursued it all the way to expertise, often by odd routes. During his early fifties, for instance, he became interested in welding, and for several years he spent his evenings down at his plant welding everything in sight: the metal trays in which the ice cream he manufactured was sent into the freezers to harden, damaged bumpers on his trucks and rusted parts of his manufacturing equipment. Sometimes, he simply welded pieces of metal together to practise his skills. He wasn't so much an inventor as a fabricator, one who created a number of factory components from scratch, occasionally to the neglect of good business and the less physical things around the place that needed tending. He fabricated ideas the same way, obsessively, and not always efficiently or accurately.

What you see in this photograph are what had become the essential instruments of his being as he approached his sixties: his right brain, his right hand, his furrowed brow—worried, perhaps, but unafraid despite the shadows, and skeptical of other people, too many of whom he'd decided were fools. This was not a despairing judgment, because he remained roundly optimistic about human possibility all his life, despite the growing density of fools he detected in the world, of which I was from time to time judged to be one.

I was afraid of him at this age even though I had entered, nominally, my adulthood. But when I look at this photograph now, the fear dissolves. What ideas were seething in his brain as he stopped to pose for this photograph? Why wasn't I more curious about what he was thinking?

Ah, wait. I know the answer to those questions. I was afraid of the ideas he had about me, or about the plans he had to make me over as a copy of himself.

But what if he was merely thinking about moonlight on new-fallen snow, or the futility of trying to influence the young?

TEN

I seldom considered my father a fun guy, even though, now that I think about it, I saw him enjoy himself innumerable times at many different things and in different ways. What I never saw was the merriness evident in this photo, likely taken in Hawaii in the early 1970s. He's got a suntan—or sunburn—and his swim trunks are rolled top and bottom, enough to expose the undersuit. He has a burger in his right hand and a Pepsi in his left. That's a flower lei around his neck, and I don't even want to speculate about what he's got on his head.

Yet in the midst of acting sillier than I ever saw him, he remains completely himself. He manufactured Pepsi-Cola in northern B.C., and on the second chair in the photo is a bottle of Canada Dry ginger ale, for which he also held the northern franchise. He was almost certainly testing them to see if they tasted the same as the stuff he bottled. It's half a decade after he sold the business, but he's still conducting these kinds of tests, and there's no way on earth there would have been a bottle of Coke in this picture, because he hated Coke and wouldn't have it in his house even in his nineties. His fidelities were few and unpredictable, but those he had were upheld without second thoughts.

This minor approximation of a lobster is also the darkest tan I saw on him until he went into a rest home in 1999 and began doing impersonations of George Hamilton IV, sitting in the sun all day long because he'd discovered, as he put it, "the sun feels good on my skin."

ELEVEN

Hartley Fawcett fondled women all his life, but he did it under strict rules—as far as we know, anyway. The fondling was limited to situations like this one: not local, the women had to be young, engaged in some sort of public entertainment, and the fondling was as you see here, advancing, in rare circumstances, only to the partial cupping of a breast. Usually it occurred as you see it here—in a posed photograph, with a last-second grab. There are a startling number of similar photos in the family archive, enough to make me laugh out loud when I found this one, the only one where you can see what's going through his mind.

The photograph was taken in Hawaii, likely by my mother. No, I don't know what happened next. The young woman, who looks a little anxious, may have slapped him, and my mother might have thought about slapping him. But more likely, what you see was the extent of it.

I know very little about what he thought about sex and equally little about what he did as a sexual being, at least until he was well into his nineties, when his inhibitions vanished and he couldn't get enough of it. He was a travelling salesman for many years, so one could speculate . . . but somehow, I doubt it. The only clue he ever gave me was when we were on that trip together into Alberta in 1983, and he asked me, out of the blue, how many women I'd been, you know, friendly with. When I named a number north of two dozen, there was dead silence. Then he said, "Well, I be go to hell."

That was the end of the conversation.

When my brother asked him what he wanted for entertainment at his hundredth birthday party, he said, without hesitating for even a second: "Belly Dancers." So my brother found two belly dancers: local girls I think, big women just a titch on the beefy side of voluptuous. My father managed to get his mitts on both of them, and he was quite a lot less restrained about it than in this picture.

TWELVE

No one has been able to explain this photograph. No one knows where it was taken, or what they were doing. Both have wigs on their heads, the decor is beyond rickety, and what's with the beads? My father's face is tanned, but his legs are dead white so they're not on some foreign vacation gone Dogpatch. And look! They're having fun. My mother has a cigarette in her left hand, something is funny off to their right, and her right hand is in his lap. A moment before, they were likely holding hands.

The point of including this photo is to suggest that domestic wars are not total, and that their life wasn't really hell, not all the time, and not even essentially. If misery shortens lives, how was it that these two got 190 years on the planet between the two of them?

Once, after I complained that staying married to anyone seemed impossible, a woman friend of mine who'd had a deeply complicated marriage asked me who it was that told me marriage was supposed to be easy. She and her husband had perpetrated all sorts of domestic mayhem on each other, including innumerable infidelities and a destructive bout of wife/husband swapping. Then they stopped, and spent years in therapy, more or less content with one another until she died of the same thing that nearly got my mother, breast cancer.

I imagine that they had their share of similar proofs-of-happiness. But somehow, I don't think they had as many as Hartley Fawcett and Rita Surry.

THIRTEEN

In September 1983, my father and I drove his big red Cadillac Coupe de Ville to northern Alberta from B.C.'s Okanagan Valley on our first and last road trip together. He was 76 years old at the time, and I was about to turn 40. I'd instigated the trip because I'd realized I knew nothing about his early life, and he responded with a characteristic combination of enthusiasm and wary suspicion about my motives after a quarter century of father-and-son mayhem.

For a glorious week we traipsed through the landscapes he'd grown up in—and gleefully abandoned—most of them in the farmland north of Edmonton. I met a dozen relatives I'd never seen or heard of before, and mostly liked them for being slightly sweeter and less aggressive than my father. We found a coal mine—a side-hill loaded with low-grade lignite he and a buddy had worked during the winter of 1930, and I saw the tiny house he was born in during the spring of 1907 along with a dozen other of his memory sites.

One afternoon, as we were driving along a rural road north of Riviere Qui Barre, he abruptly pulled the Cadillac off the road and into a grassy field. Given the car's weight and the black gumbo of the surrounding fields, I was immediately wondering how we were going to get out again, but beneath the layer of sod was an old gravel road, and, 100 metres along, a small, broken-down bridge. We climbed out of the car and walked over to the edge of the old bridge. A tiny creek ran beneath it, fouled with gumbo.

"Well, I be go to hell," my father said, pointing off in the distance. "It's still standing."

I wasn't quite sure what he was talking about. There was a farmhouse, and beyond it in the fields, a ramshackle barn. "What am I looking at?" I asked.

"That barn," he said. "I built that. My brother Alex and I. And this bridge here. We built that, too. Took us a whole summer. We cut and bucked the timbers ourselves from a grove of big tamaracks that was—" he waved his finger uncertainly to the northeast of the barn "—over there."

I ducked back into the car for my camera, and by the time I had it primed he was standing calmly in front of the bridge, unzipping his trousers to take a leak. So I shot this photograph, the truest and most candid realization I was ever to get of him and his attitude toward the past, including his own.

FOURTEEN

Rita Surry wasn't a sporting woman. She neither played nor followed sports, unless it was the Stanley Cup finals or the World Series, and even then she'd only watch if someone else was with her. She wasn't interested in fitness until her geriatric years, when she took in a few exercise classes, more for the company than anything else. She wasn't much of a swimmer, either, although, unlike my father, she knew how.

Yet she liked the outdoors, liked to camp with family or with others, and even enjoyed the trips to Arizona and other points south my father insisted on in the several years after he came home one day with an absurdly shiny 28-foot Airstream trailer hooked to the back of his Cadillac.

I never once saw her with a fishing rod in her hands—except in this photo, taken on Babine Lake in northeastern B.C during the early 1960s. It is a perfect demonstration of her idea of how sports ought to go. She is fast asleep, but note the two-handed grip on the rod, and the carefully placed reel knob resting between her index and middle finger to alert her if one of those 5-pound steelheads Babine Lake was famous for hit the lure.

She was a woman who could walk and chew gum at the same time, but she preferred not to let on she was good at it, and never got proud about being able to when others couldn't. She had another trick, this one learned: if she was bored, she took a nap. But even when she did, she had, as you can see, her wits about her.

FIFTEEN

Look at this guy! He doesn't get along with his wife, giant corporations squash him and steal his business, his sons desert him, he's lived his entire life on the chilly margin of civilization working 12-hour days. Where does he get a grin like that? What's his secret?

I'm beginning to get it: *Carpe Diem*; locate the sugar in whatever you're doing, wherever you are; be ruthless in your pursuit of it.

In this picture he's in a sugar cane field in Hawaii, a place he liked more than most. But I've seen that same look a thousand other times: when he recognized the solution to a balky compressor on one of his freezer trucks he'd been working on for three hours, and I've seen it as he bit into a peach he'd grown himself.

In the wilderness of the self, we're all miserable: we don't get exactly what we want, other people don't do what we'd like them to, no one gives us the uncritical love we deserve. The right ship never comes in, not really. The pirates steal most of the gold and the rhinestones, the rats have been living in the hold the entire voyage, raising their own.

So you learn how to live in the moment, amongst its particularities, and you deploy your will to shift whatever details you can to your advantage. Or at least, that's what this man did. His happiness arose from the immediate pleasure or the immediate labour, not from the contemplation of an ideal self or in the sullen arithmetic of perfection, at which we all fail. Nothing was needed to make him happy because he was instantly there: he willed it so, and persisted in that will.

SIXTEEN

My father figured out that life is a mess at a much earlier age than I did. He never let the shadow of it affect him, or if it did get to him, he didn't let on. He put whatever he could in order, and didn't whine when it overwhelmed him, except to mutter about all the jackasses who liked to get in his way. At the end of his life he grew almost tender when he recognized something or someone coming to grief. He'd laugh ruefully, shake his head as if life was an inescapable series of practical jokes that had to be endured so one could get back to the serious business deals that were there to be made: his definition of honey. The mess rarely soured his disposition for long, and it never, ever broke through the steely optimism that was the core of his character: life was good even if there were people out there who didn't contribute to it.

"You know," he told me once, apropos of nothing, "you can always work on something."

I had no idea what he was talking about, no inkling that he was imparting a profound truth it would take a quarter century to decipher. I'd been infected by my generation's conviction that work was to be avoided, and that what really counted was how firm a grip I could get on the dials of the entertainment channels the World Machines were then creating to lock us permanently in the realm of the unproductively inane. I thought he had some project lined up for me I wouldn't want to do: collecting interesting rocks for a new retaining wall in his garden, or helping him sell whatever miracle product had lately caught his fancy. It took far too long before I realized that he was talking about the same things Jean-Paul Sartre had on his mind when he used the term "project," or Albert Camus when he talked about "absurdity."

SEVENTEEN

As the eldest daughter in a dysfunctional but highly articulate family, before she was out of her teens my mother understood very well that life is a mess. After that, I don't think she was ever quite able to forget it. It occasionally soured her, but sometimes, when things did make sense, she gathered in the order like a farmer harvesting the first ripe tomatoes of the season, savouring each moment of sense before it turned back into the foul swill that everything ends as.

Late in her life she consciously sought respites from the mess. She liked to sit atop the hill above the lakeside home my father built in the early 1970s, and she'd spend hours gazing out across the often-glassy waters of Skaha Lake watching the transport trucks chugging into town along the west side of the lake.

I don't know what thoughts went through her head while she was up there. Unless it was spring, that is. That was when she climbed up there almost daily to pick the wild asparagus that grew all through the abandoned apricot orchards, humming to herself as she picked.

Salt and Cinnamon

I T STRUCK ME, in the mid-1990s that I'd never asked either of my parents what they thought about life and about their place in it. The truth was that I'd never been very interested, and the idea that they had "inner lives" was alien and vaguely threatening. In part this is a "natural" carry-over of the authority parents have during one's childhood, but in my case it was at least partly because my father was always telling me exactly what he thought, then trying to force me to agree with him, and finding it incomprehensible when I had alternate views, which I did have about virtually everything.

But now I wanted to get some of their thoughts onto the record, not so much because I was suddenly filled with curiosity, but because their grandchildren and great-grandchildren might some-day wonder what their ancestors liked and disliked, and what they thought about the human condition. I drew up a list of about 40 questions, starting with simple stuff like, "What's your favourite colour or vegetable or fabric?" After that, I moved on to fundamental questions like, "Is your life a success?" and "How important is sexual happiness?"

It seemed an outlandish thing to ask one's parents point-blank what they liked and disliked about the world and what they thought about life's big issues. I could find no one who'd done anything like it in a systematic way. When I told several friends what I intended to do, most responded with an "oh, wow," that let me know they weren't about to rush off to draw up a list of their own questions.

As the decade began to wind down, it became apparent that I'd better get going if I was to have these conversations. My father was already in his nineties, and my mother's health, in her late eighties, was beginning to fail. So in September 1998, I cornered her while she was visiting Toronto, and got her to agree to answer "some" questions. I didn't say how many, or what they were going to be about. She wasn't terrifically enthused, but after a bit of wrangling, she agreed to it.

We sat down on the backyard deck of my house on the second-last day of her two-week visit. She'd come because she wanted her tenth grandchild, my then 14-month-old daughter, Hartlea, to know her paternal grandmother.

The visit had gone very well. Grandmother and granddaughter quickly bonded, and the small anxiety my mother's growing physical handicaps must have been raising in her mind about the practicality of a relationship with a toddler had been sweetly resolved. Hartlea's walking pace was perfectly tuned to my mother's, and they spent hours together happily exploring the streetscapes in our neighbourhood. The relationship had been made, my mother had a sense of little Hartlea's character, and she'd relaxed, her mind at peace.

I was the anxious one, actually. Several years before, I'd made a number of tape recordings of her reminiscences about the past, with the thought of collecting them in the same sort of life history I'd made for my father 15 years before. In the tapes I made with her, she'd recounted anecdote upon story after fable for me, but they'd all been oddly unsatisfying. She was so seamless a raconteur that the stories dramatized events without revealing very much, if anything, of her. Her recall of her life was utterly unlike my father's reminiscences, which all led back to a single philosophical point of reference: his business successes, and why I and everyone else ought to emulate him. Her reminiscences were pure plot—and therefore pure fabrication, complete with the telling, but disconnected from any deeper issues of character or values. For posterity, I wanted a record that would reveal at least something of what she believed about human life and the things about it that troubled her.

It was late in the afternoon before we got down to it, sitting across from one another at a round metal deck table with a pot of tea and a tape recorder in the warm September sunlight. As we settled in, I realized that the two of us had been talking all my life, but we'd never once talked this way. She told stories—usually about others—or she gave situational and practical advice. But she was elusive about herself and evasive when asked to talk on terms not of her choosing. It hadn't ever been that one or the other of us consciously controlled the agenda when we talked. It was more an issue of having comfortably worked out our relative roles with one another. She'd never been one to burden her kids with her thoughts, and as the youngest of her children and the one on whom she'd lavished the most attention, I'd let myself think that she didn't have an inner life. She, underplaying her hand as she always did, had allowed me to think whatever I wanted for nearly 50 years.

I clicked on the tape recorder, and to get her attention, I shuffled the sheet of questions I had in front of me. "I've got about 40 questions here," I said. "So why don't we start with some of the easy ones. Let's try this: What's your favourite season?"

She looked puzzled for a moment. "What's my favourite sea-soning? That's rather hard to say. I can't imagine life without salt or cinnamon."

"I don't think that's quite the question," I said, laughing. "But it's a good answer. Salt and cinnamon. I've got to write that down."

She frowned. Was I playing with her? Wasn't this supposed to be serious? "Well," she said, "I do love anything with cinnamon in it. And what would life be without salt. It'd be like life without sex."

"I was asking you what your favourite *season* was."

Her turn to laugh. "Oh, for God's sake," she said. "I thought you wanted to know my favourite seasoning. That's funny. Well, my favourite season is autumn. It's so rich and fulfilled, and oh, I don't know. It just seems to me the ultimate harvest time, I guess."

We went through the other easy ones. Favourite vegetable: asparagus, preferably wild; Fish? She liked salmon, but having spent most of her adult life in the B.C. Interior, distinguished it from seafood, which she enjoyed more. For that, it was orange roughy. She described it this way: "splendid. It comes from Australia, and sole is nothing compared to it. It's like sole but it has body. It doesn't fall apart on you, which I don't like."

I asked her a question I thought I knew the answer to because I bought it for her most Christmases: What was her favourite perfume?

"I prefer 4711," she said. "I used to like Chanel 22. But older women shouldn't wear strong perfume. It makes them cheap, I think. So Chanel 22 is now too harsh for me. Too, ah . . . indel-icate. It was good when I was young and flirty."

She looked directly into my eyes to make sure I'd gotten the message. "My ambition in life now is to grow old gracefully. And 4711 is graceful."

I made the appropriate mental note: No more Chanel 22. Had she been giving it away, or did she have a cupboard full of it somewhere in the Penticton house?

On we went: favourite flower? carnations (a surprise, I assumed it would be roses); favourite tree? maple, because of their autumn colours; favourite colour? rose, and yellow; favourite fabric? satin. I could see she was getting a little bored, so I began to pop more complicated questions.

"What," I asked, "do you think life is for? Does life have any purpose?"

She was silent for a long moment. "Do you mean personally, or in general?"

"Either, or rather, both."

"Well," she said, "it's rather a difficult question because it has so many aspects."

I could feel her scrambling on the unfamiliar ground. "For instance," she said after another pause, "a man and a woman have different purposes in life. Basically, I think most women want to be mothers. Men may want children to bear their name or continue the race I guess, but women want children because, well, they make you *whole*. I think they bring us the greatest happiness in life, depending of course on your outlook."

"If you're a professional woman, for instance"—she glanced into the house where Leanna was fussing with some papers in the kitchen—"possibly not. But when I look at you, or at your brother, or the twins, I understand that life is going to go on. It doesn't end with me. And that's everything."

"So the purpose of life is to continue life?"

"Yes, I think so," she said, gazing directly at me. "Life is its own purpose."

"Okay," I said. "Next question: Does God exist? And if so, in what form? I mean, do you think that God is a guy up there somewhere, sitting on a throne, dreaming up horrible things to do to us?"

She cleared her throat and laughed, accepting that this line of questions was going to go on, and letting me know she thought it was absurd that I was asking her about such things.

"I've never analyzed what God is," she said. "But you know, religion is purely a matter of faith. I asked our minister in Prince George about it once, and he said that sometimes he'd had questions. So it's what you choose to believe. There's no proof or certainty."

I let that answer hang for a moment because its sophistication surprised me more than a little, and because I was hoping she'd go on.

"When I had cancer," she said, "I said to God, if you let me live and see my children finish high school, get married, and start successful lives where they've got somebody else to love them besides me, I promise that I'll try to help other people as long as I live. And I've done that—because I made a promise to something that is real. It wasn't an imaginary something in the clouds that I made that promise to. And I think because of that, when I had the second bout of cancer, I never questioned whether I'd survive."

For a moment I was thrown by the idea of my mother talking to God. She'd told me several times in the past she didn't believe in God. Then the second datum registered: second bout of cancer? When did that happen? And why didn't I know about it?

I had to collect myself to prompt the next question: "So this God you talked to was more an embodiment of what goes around comes around rather than the giant guy in the white robe, inflicting natural disasters and sending people plagues of boils, right?"

She tried to give me a stern look, but lost it to a smile. Then she composed herself.

"I've really never tried to analyze what God might *look* like. God has never needed to look like anything. God just is. I mean, how can anyone look at a beautiful tree, or all the beautiful flowers, the wonderful colours of nature and not see something behind it. What would the world be without beauty? So, where did it come from? It had to start somewhere. I think that's why people say God created the world—because it's beautiful."

She was warming up to what we were doing, so I pressed it. "You're saying that beautiful things have to come from something beyond us? That they're not random?"

"I'm saying that life didn't just appear out of nothing. That doesn't mean it's all good, though. The world is like your father says it is: there are good people and there are bad people. But I would never try to ram any of this down other people's throats the way he does. I decided with you children that I would take you to church, but that what you did with it, once you got old enough to think for yourselves, was up to you. It wasn't for me to say what you should believe about these things. I have my own private beliefs, and they're actually quite different to that of a lot of people I know. It's a private thing. Just mine. Sometimes I drive along the street and see something that disturbs me, and I'll say, 'Well, what do you think of that, God?'"

That made me laugh out loud, and she did, too, albeit sheepishly. "Maybe it's a weakness that I need something to lean on," she said. "But I don't see it so."

"I don't think it's silly," I assured her, and changed my tack slightly to let her expand on it in a different way. "What's the most important thing in life, then?"

The question seemed to stop her in her tracks. "That's a toughie," she said. There was a long silence as she considered how to answer.

"Here's what I think," she said, finally. "The most important thing in life—to me—is family. My family. It's so important that we belong to one another, and that we love each other. It doesn't matter whether what we do is perfect or imperfect. What matters is that we're still family."

"There're several possible ways to understand family," I said. "One is family in the sense of 'us against them.'"

"No, no," she said. "Not that way. That just starts wars."

"Then there's family for the purposes of living a good and decent life. Are you saying that the best way to lead a good and decent life is through the family?"

She considered this for a moment.

"That's close to what I mean," she said. "But let me explain how this works for someone my age. This latest granddaughter, for instance. She's a perfect little thing in and of herself, but she's also partly me, and mine. I feel that way with all of you, including the great-grandchildren. They're my family, and they're part of what is me."

"Your sense of family is mostly in the present," I said. "It doesn't go very deep into the past, does it?"

I wondered if she'd see this as a criticism, but she didn't. It was an opening to something else she wanted to make clear.

"My sense of family doesn't go into the past because the family I grew up in didn't have a sense of belonging to anything larger than themselves as individuals. In that respect, I'm different from the rest of them. That was the difference between me and your uncle Ronald, for instance. I was the one who had a family, but he only had himself, even though he'd had two wives, and three children. He thought what I had was wonderful, but he didn't really understand it. You know, he once said, 'Family isn't important to me, but at the back of my mind I've known, all my life, that my sister Rita was there. That she was mine, even if no one else was.'"

"Dad's family doesn't have a strong sense of what you're talking about, either, does it?"

"No," she said, flatly. "None at all."

"Do you think that not being interested in family and kin is a British thing? I've always noticed that my ethnic friends here—the Italians, or Leanna's family—are a lot more conscious of who their ancestors are, and where they came from. Our families go back maybe a generation, and that's it."

She looked up into the trees, as if considering whether what I'd suggested might be true. For a moment her face went blank.

"No," she said, and hesitated again. "I think it's a matter of individual families and individuals. I was raised exactly the same way as my brothers and sisters, and none of them had the strong feeling about family I've always had. I think maybe my sister, Enid, had it with her kids, but it didn't extend any further. I don't know why they didn't have it, but there you are."

"Do you think this might have something to do with the fact that you were the one who got the farthest away from the family you were born into? There you and Dad were, in a sense, out there in the B.C. wilderness, and there wasn't anybody to help. So you had to invent a new kind of family."

"Maybe," she said. "But even before we moved to British Columbia, I kept in touch with both my family and his. I was always the only one who wrote letters to all my brothers and sisters, and to my mother. That impulse comes from within. If you haven't got that instinct, you just don't have it."

"But where does it come from in the first place?"

She laughed, signalling that she'd taken this one as far as she could. "I don't know everything. That's your job."

"Let's change the subject, then," I said. "How about this question: Which person most influenced you in your life?"

Just for a moment I caught a flicker of panic in her eyes. Then she settled herself in her chair. "Someone completely outside the family," she said.

"You're being mysterious. Who are you talking about?"

She laughed again, but her eyes were serious, and a little distant. "This person gave me the courage to go on living when I . . ." Her voice trailed off as she stared into the trees across the alley.

"Cancer," she said after a long pause, "is a very frightening thing." She paused again, rolling her tongue and swallowing, as if recalling the fear she'd felt anew. "And as perhaps you know, your father had nothing to offer me emotionally. I was pretty damned scared until this man gave me the assurance I needed that I was going to be alright. And I believed him. If I hadn't, I don't think I'd be sitting here today."

I scrambled for a way to get her to clarify something she clearly thought I was supposed to know all about and didn't. Well, I thought, let's go through the front door.

"Who are we talking about, exactly? You've lost me."

She named a man I'd met once or twice, one of my father's business suppliers. "It all started innocently enough," she said. "After my breast was removed, which you know all about, I was there in that hospital all by myself, not knowing if I was going to live or die, and he came in and sat with me."

"Go on," I said. "Tell the story."

"There isn't really a story," she said. "He was there when I needed him, sometimes just talking about what was going on in the world, and sometimes talking directly about what was happening to me. He gave me the same message every time."

"What message?" I said, feeling perfectly stupid at not being able to lead the story for her.

"That I was going to be fine, that it was just a medical procedure, and that *everything* (she put a heavy emphasis on the word) was going to be okay."

"That was a very kind thing to do," I said, still lost.

"He was there," she said, "in a way your father never was. I had to go back down to Vancouver for radiation treatments several times after that, and there he was then, too. And a few years later, he came to Prince George."

"This must have been when I met him," I said, trying hard to picture him—and failing.

I could see that she didn't want to tell me the whole story, and I was feeling uncomfortable about its implications: Was my mother telling me she'd had an affair? I moved on to the next question, not quite sure whether I was being discreet or cowardly.

This was a question to which I was pretty sure I had the answer: "What would you say your life's most important accomplishment has been?"

No hesitation on this, and her face brightened. "Ah," she said. "My children. I feel so fulfilled when I see them. Maybe I'm just a homebody, but that's what it is."

I thought about pointing out that her children are fairly flawed and ordinary, but telling her that would have stolen some of her pleasure. Why do that? She thinks we're wonderful, even if we know better. Then it occurred to me that she did know how flawed we are—better than we do—and that she didn't care. What mattered to her was that we're all alive, and all of us have given her grandchildren. She didn't ever ask much more from us. I read out the next question, still thinking about her answer to that one.

"Which gender is superior, and why?"

She frowned, but answered immediately. "Neither, as far as I'm concerned. Each individual has to be judged on their own merit.

You can't classify this one as superior, or that one, just because they were born male or female . . ."

"I guess what I'm asking is what natural advantages the different genders have."

Her expression shifted. This nuance interested her, and she thought about it for a moment before answering. "I think, well, that a mother gets to mold her children when they're babies and beyond that. She's got to be there for them, and they've got to know she's there for them. And maybe a father—if he's a good father—has a stronger influence on them when they're older."

"That," I said, "would make you both my mother and my father."

"Don't be silly," she said, and laughed. I could see I'd pleased her. But once I'd said it, I wasn't certain it was true. Sure, I was always closer to her than to my father, but how much had she influenced me? She'd never much tried to after I reached the age of 12 or so. She was much better at enjoying me, and at times, teasing me. She'd teased me all through my adolescence as a way of cautioning me against the goofy teenaged stunts that could have gotten me killed. It worked surprisingly well, too. I'd walked away from more than a few situations because I could sense her laughter coming.

"Here's one I've never asked you," I said. "How would you describe your politics?"

"My what?"

"Your politics."

"Hah!" she spat out. "I've deliberately kept clear of politics because I haven't agreed with your father about *his* politics. And publicly disagreeing with him was hell on earth."

"So you're saying you're really a communist."

We both knew that wasn't true, but curiously, she didn't deny it.

"I have my own private thoughts about politics," she said. "But like I said, I've had to stay clear of talking about them because I got into trouble whenever I did."

"Did you find yourself characteristically *not* in agreement with Dad?"

She laughed, not quite merrily. "Yes," she said. "Always. Unfortunately. You know he was always accusing me of being against him, but the truth is that we couldn't ever have political discussions because if I didn't agree with everything he said, he accused me of being against him. That's a shame, because you learn so much by discussing things. But with your father I never could express my political opinions because in his mind they were simply personal attacks on him. So politics was just something I didn't talk about, after a while."

"That doesn't seem fair," I said.

"It wasn't. But I kept my mouth shut to keep the peace, because that was more important."

"Okay," I said. "Another question: Where is your home? If you were to go home in the deepest possible sense, where would it be?"

Her eyes narrowed, as if she was wondering if I was laying some sort of trap. She couldn't see one, and relaxed. "You know, it didn't matter to me what city I was living in. What mattered was where my family—my kids—were. I was always home when I was with my kids."

"But given that, in which city did you feel most at home?"

"Oh, then it would be Prince George. That's where you all grew up and that's where you were mine entirely."

"Was that because those were the years when you were in the 'big part' of your life?"

"Yes," she said. "I guess that's what it was. I didn't think of it that way at the time, but that's what it was."

I found myself recalling a strange story she'd once told me about those early days in Prince George. It was late August 1944, so there was the deep ripeness of summer. The war was going well after the Normandy invasion, and she'd taken all four of us downtown for a walk, me in a carriage, since I was barely four months old.

The Fall Assizes were about to start, so the town was full of people, many of them aboriginal families of those who were about to go on trial. As she was approaching the main intersection of town, Third Avenue and George Street, passing along the large display windows of Ben Baird Men's Wear on the southwest corner, there was a minor earthquake tremor, strong enough for her to see the window glass bulge and undulate above my carriage. But the tremor passed, the windows didn't shatter, and the order of her gentle universe resettled.

When she told me this story, her point seemed like an odd one: that she always felt safe in Prince George. She'd been surrounded by the alien and mostly uncommunicative families of Carriers, no doubt by drunken loggers, she'd been threatened by an earthquake and crazily shimmering store windows, and *this* made her feel safe? From what? What was the threat?

She wasn't about to articulate the threat that had made Prince George seem like a haven to her, but now it was clear to me. The morass her family constituted for her; the grudges held, the overindulged emotions and appetites; the sheer muck of being. She'd gotten herself and her children away from it, and she felt, for the first time in her life, safe enough to make a different kind of world for them.

She was drifting away into a reverie, and it was my fault. I'd been pushing my private agenda, and been getting the answers I wanted. But as I watched her, I recognized that many of the answers were more complicated than they appeared, and more complicated than I'd expected—and that the questions ran deeper for her than for me.

"When," I said, "were you most happy in your life?"

"Oh, that's easy," she said. "When all you kids were at home. I mean, really, I had a wonderful girlhood. From the time I reached my teens I had the most marvellous group of girlfriends. We went to new places all the time, explored things. And I kept in touch with them all our lives. But they're all gone, now. Inez was the last to go. She and I were much closer than I was to my sisters, in a way."

"So ages 12 to 25 was also a good period in your life."

"No, it was more ages 16 to 25. I really wasn't very happy until about 16, and began to get away from my family a little." She frowned, as if she didn't like the implications, and shifted the subject. "You know, both your father and I have lost nearly all our old friends. You suffer the loss, but you forget that time passes. You know what I mean."

I didn't but I could feel my skin starting to crawl at the thought of my own friends dying. "What's the worst thing that ever happened to you?" I asked.

There was silence. Then she had it, or rather, it had her. Her eyes clouded. "I . . . I think," she said, "it was the day I found out that I had cancer. That was quite a blow. It was in the summer, and it changed my whole way of looking at the world."

"Changed it how?"

"After that happened, a coloured leaf, say, or a flower, became the most wonderful things imaginable. Before, I just sort of saw the world around me as if it was wallpaper, and went about my business. But after, I knew I might die, and it made everyday things precious."

She laughed again, but it was dry, a hedge against the emotions that were washing through her. "An experience like that changes you. It either defeats you, or you become a better, stronger person. I like to think I did become a better, stronger person."

She wasn't eager to stay with that memory, still traumatic to her, so I let it go.

"What's the second worst thing that ever happened to you?" I asked.

No pause to think about this one. "When your father took off a couple of times it was pretty awful," she said, with a quick, rigid laugh. "That was a blow to my ego."

I was startled at the shift. "I guess it must have been," I said. "I've never thought of it that way before."

She was willing to explore this catastrophe. "I mean," she said, "I thought, my God. How am I going to deal with this? But you know, you couldn't blame him entirely. I had to take some of the blame myself."

"Wasn't that last mess set off by Ron Surry's presence? I have to admit you kind of brought that one on yourself. A little bit, anyway."

"Well, I would never have had your uncle come there the way he did, but your father was all for it. He said, 'Oh wonderful, have your brother here.' At the back of it was the thought, aha! She can go live with him, and I can get rid of her. He told me that, actually. He said, 'What do you think I had your brother come out here for?' You see, your father can be a very devious person."

Over the years I'd thought of my father in various uncomplimentary ways—as harsh, insensitive and occasionally as cruel, but devious? I'd seen him *try* to be devious, mostly during family card games. He was the world's most incompetent cheater. I'd spent a half-dozen Christmas night Rumoli games tucking cards under my seat while everyone was focused on his lame attempts to do the same.

I looked up, and saw that she was waiting for a response. "Yes," I said. "I suppose he can be, but only in a short-sighted kind of way. He doesn't think very far ahead or very deeply when it comes to personal matters."

The hint of a sneer twisted her lips, and then she plunged on. "You do know," she said, her voice dropping a little in case anyone was listening, "that the basis of that affair he had with that woman was that he'd become impotent? He was on all this medication for his heart. But he blamed me for the impotence.

"'You don't inspire me anymore,' he'd say. 'You're just an old hag.' And I said, 'Please, Hartley, go and discuss it with your doctor. I'm sure it's your medication.' But he said, 'No, no bloody way.' And then, of course, he goes off with this woman who is a nurse. And, of course, sure enough she tells him the same thing.

"So the next thing I heard was, 'Mommy, can I come home?' It wasn't Mommy's fault at all. But anyway, to have your husband walk out on you is an awful blow to your ego. The first time he left he said it was your grandmother's fault."

I must have looked startled, so she took a deep breath and explained.

"He left me twice. Both times there was another woman involved. The first time was while we were still in Prince George, and that time he even went so far as to buy a house for his girlfriend in White Rock. The reason I found out was because I was keeping all his accounts, and I found myself writing cheques to make the mortgage payments on the house. So I went to see the woman— she was a social worker living in Prince George—when he went up to Grande Prairie on business. He didn't know until quite a while afterward I'd talked to her."

She paused, as if reliving the details had become acutely painful.

"Go on," I said. "I probably ought to know about this."

"You see, he'd just sold his business, and the word around town was that he was quite a wealthy man. This woman had a little house, and had put it up for sale, and he came across her because he was looking for property to buy. Meanwhile I was cleaning up the accounts receivable on his business after he'd sold it, and they were a mess. I had to work backward about four months because there were nothing but mistakes—he'd been doing it by himself. So I was working about eight or ten hours a day on this, and your

grandmother was staying with us, bless her heart, and she was trying to talk to him and entertain him, and naturally that was driving
him crazy. Part of what set things off was that he had nothing to
do. The people who'd bought the plant had told him to stop coming around. So he was at loose ends, and ripe for something. And I
had no time to go anywhere with him because I had to get these
account books cleaned up for him.

"The next thing I knew he'd gotten this girlfriend, and he'd
bought a house for her. So anyway, as I said, I dropped around to
chat with her. I'd talked to old Hub King, the family lawyer, about
it before I went, and he'd said, 'Well, the man is nuts.' So I went
to this woman and I said, 'You know, Hartley, my husband, who
you've decided to take off with, is under a lot of stress, and the day
he moves out of our house, his lawyer and I are going to have him
declared mentally incompetent—which Hub King had promised
he was going to try to do—and so he won't have any money that we
don't give him. And I will never divorce him while he's ill.'"

"That was devious of you."

She laughed at the turnabout. "Maybe it was," she said. "But
there was a lot at stake. Anyway, when he came home from Grande
Prairie and went bouncing over to see her, she dumped him. He'd
already bought the house, and they'd both been down on a couple
of weekends to look it over. You didn't know that? He ran away on
me twice."

While I was trying to think of something to say, she went on.
"You see," she said, "your father needs somebody to build him up
all the time. Or he needs someone to lord it over so he can feel . . .
ah, I don't know what he needs, and I guess I've stopped caring. You
do know the girls and Ron were very cross with me the second time
I took him back, don't you? They said, 'You're an idiot. You know
he's not going to change.'"

"Did he change?"

"I don't know," she said. "I think I stopped caring about it some-where along the line. I kept things together because I thought our family wouldn't be the same if your father and I divorced. You'd be going here, you'd be going there, and *that* wasn't my family. The family needed us to be together, so . . . I don't know. I just don't know."

She took a small sip of tea, stared out across the small garden, and waited for me to get her out of it. Had staying been a good idea? On her terms, yes: family was everything. But all the divorces amongst her four children suggested another possible way of see-ing things. Should I tell her this? No. I did what you're supposed to do in difficult moments: I made a joke of it.

"I can remember the second affair pretty clearly," I said. "The Grecian Formula 16 he used to make himself look younger, and how ridiculous it was when it turned his hair bright yellow."

"Well," she said, not buying the deflection, "I knew how to han-dle the second one better than the first. He came to see me—and slept with me—the day he moved down to White Rock. I was sick with the flu, and he had a key and came in. I was still doing the bookkeeping and he had to come and sign some cheques. So, before he went down there he stopped in—he'd already taken a truckload down filled with furniture—and now he had his car with a U-Haul on the back, and he parked it in the carport and stayed there that night, and then he took off anyway the next morning. But ten days later he was back.

"This time I said, 'You can go to hell,' but of course I didn't mean it. Anyway, marriage wasn't heaven. There were a lot of diffi-cult things that happened."

"So, how important is sexual happiness?"

She gazed at me as if she didn't quite understand the question. "Very," she said, after a moment. "But your father doesn't know what sexual equality is. Sex was all for him. And if you tried to do anything, you were a slut. He's a terrible prude. He didn't know what sex is about, not for a woman. He didn't understand that it wasn't just for his physical release. That it could be joyous. Providing . . . Well, it takes two. And it rises and falls—it doesn't stay static, ever. But, if you haven't got it . . . I don't think anyone can be completely happy without it. I think when it's mutual it's what makes a marriage . . . sometimes. Companionship is important, too. Very, very important."

I could see she was unhappy with the way this was going, so I changed directions—or so I thought. "What's the most surprising thing you've ever done?" I asked.

This got me another thoughtful pause. I thought she was trying to decide what had surprised her most, but I was wrong. She had it instantly.

"I had my own chance to take off, once," she said. "It startled me that I had the guts to say no when I wanted to say yes with every bit of me."

"And you said no anyway? That surprised you?"

"Well, it surprised me that I had something in me that *had* to do the right thing. The other person came to the same conclusion. So, we decided, together. And the funny part of it is, I've never been sorry, and yet I've never lost the memory of that moment when I had that choice. So really, I've had it both ways. Maybe if we'd said yes to it, who knows? It might have ended up with disillusionment and unhappiness. Family is so, so much a part of me, and yet I would have been lost if that moment had never happened. But then I wouldn't have been completely happy without all of you."

"So you're saying that life sometimes presents us with situations where there's no right choice?"

"Yes. Not often, but yes, it happens. And the choice he and I made was the right choice, for both of us. It was a situation where we couldn't win."

She refilled her teacup from the pot—Leanna had freshened it—and leaned back. "It would have been glorious, though. For a while, at least. But you know, you never lose the feeling. The most amazing part of it, as far as I'm concerned, when I say you never lose it, is that over the years when I got utterly desperate, in my dreams this moment came back and gave me the courage to go on. It still does. It's like it happened yesterday, and we're still there, you know? So maybe I did the right thing. I haven't ever really regretted the decision. Not often, anyway."

"Is your life a success?"

"I think it is. I don't feel like I'm a failure. I really don't. I may be a jack of all trades and master of none, but I think I've done—not all but—many of the things I wanted to."

"What did you accomplish that you didn't think you'd be able to?"

This got a laugh without a trace of cynicism in it. "Sticking around as long as I have," she said.

I felt a pang when she said this. There was a powerful current of anxiety in it, and a smaller one of guilt. It had never really occurred to me during those years that she was in distress, nor that she would not be as she'd always been: permanent, there forever.

"I guess," I said, "when you had cancer that first time, you didn't think you'd be around forever. I mean, you may have thought you'd survive it, but you didn't think you'd live as long a life as you have."

"No, I didn't," she said, and giggled.

"What else didn't you think you could do?"

"Well, this is my silly sense of humour. Most people wouldn't think they were successes, but they were my successes."

"What are they?"

"I think I've been good to many people and I've had a lot of wonderful friends. As a girl growing up, mostly because we lived in the country for so long, I never thought I'd have these continuing friendships. When your father and I lived in Camrose, for instance, I made two friends there, and we corresponded until they both died. One of them later visited your grandmother every week for the 15 years she was there. She never missed a week."

"What is it about the loyalty of others that surprises you? It isn't like you didn't earn it."

"I suppose maybe I did. But it still surprises me."

"Time for a harder question: What did you fail at that you wanted to achieve?"

"I'd like to have been a poet, I'd like to have been a writer like you, maybe . . ." I could see her rejecting this as she said it. "I'd just like to have excelled at *something*, and I never did. I would like to have done just one thing in an exceptional way."

"You were exceptional at family-building, weren't you?"

Her eyes brightened, then darkened. "Oh, yes," she said, barely audibly. "I guess so, but I meant . . . I would like to have played the piano, but I didn't have the talent. Just one thing I wanted to really do well. And I didn't have it."

"It's okay, Mum," I said. "You did a lot of things well. Many more things than you can see, and I'm not just talking about your recipe for shepherd's pie."

She smiled at this, and seemed to relax.

"So let me ask you this," I said. "What do you think constitutes a good life?"

"Achievement," she answered. "Companionship. And love. Not necessarily in that order."

This was a painful admission for her, admitting that she never got enough of those things. Not the first for herself, and not the last two from my father. As I sat there I recalled an elderly couple we'd seen together on the Skaha Lake boardwalk the last time I was in Penticton. I'd taken her down so we could walk through the autumn leaves—one of her favourite things—and we were sitting on a bench beside the boardwalk. The couple, in their eighties, had been holding hands as they strolled along the lake. Watching them, my mother broke into tears.

"So tell me this," I said. "Is life worth the trouble?"

"Yes," she said, unequivocally. "I'm glad I've lived. I'm glad I'm me."

"If you had it to do over again, what things would you change?"

Her face went still. "Well," she said, "we don't know ahead of time what companion we're choosing for life. And how can you know? So I don't know if I'd made a different choice that it might not have been worse. But beyond that, I don't think there are many things I'd do differently if I could. I always wanted to be a nurse, but that wasn't possible because of your grandmother's tuberculosis. And in a way, I've fulfilled that desire by volunteering at the hospital all these years."

"What things from the past do you miss most?"

For a moment, she seemed puzzled by the question. "I don't really think there's any specific thing I miss because possessions were never very important to me. So I can't say I feel devastated by anything that's gone. I do miss your grandmother's sense of humour. You know, it's odd. If something amusing happens even today, I still hear her chuckle. Everyone forgot what a fine sense of humour she had."

I could sense that she was tiring, and so I fired off the next question: "Is it our duty to take care of others?"

"It's a little ambiguous when you say 'others,'" she said.

"Well, it's an ambiguous question. I guess I'm asking whether we're our brothers' keepers?"

Her face hardened. "Some of our brothers' keepers, anyway. But not all."

"Where do you draw the line?"

"I think you help people when they're desperate or lost. But you keep your eyes open, because needy people are often out of control, and they can be ruthless and cruel."

"Does love conquer all?"

She gave me a calculating look. "No."

"What does it conquer?"

She laughed aloud. "A lot of things," she said, almost gaily. "Common sense, most of the time. It's also true that life would be unbearable without love. But there are other things that are necessary besides love."

"Would you say that love does conquer life's emptiness?"

"Yes," she said. "Oh, yes, a certain kind of love does. And that's enough."

"Why did you succeed at the things your brothers and sisters each failed miserably at? I mean, basically, at personal happiness."

"I think I was designed to be a happy person, whereas my brothers and sisters were so filled with themselves and knowing everything that they didn't have time to enjoy the small things that make people happy."

"Wait a minute," I said. "I'm not sure what you mean by this."

"You know, in my own private mind I thought they were each brilliantly intelligent, but they were, well, *oversexed*. All of them. I didn't see it until I was older, but my father was like that, too. And his brother, Uncle Vin, took Aunt Blanche to Paris on their honeymoon in the 1890s, and spent every night of their honeymoon chasing prostitutes. He was sort of the black sheep of the family anyway. That's why he came out to the United States. His family refused to speak to him for 20 years."

"I remember Uncle Vin as a kindly old man who tied different fruit to his trees to impress us when we visited."

"Well, good and evil are usually mixed together in people. Uncle Vin had some wonderful qualities. But when he was a younger man he liked to cheat on his wife, and a lot of other things you don't need to know about."

"Where do you think those sorts of urges came from?"

"I don't know. But that side of the family was obsessed with sex. Father had eight children, two with his first wife, and then six children with your grandmother, bang, bang, bang, bang."

"A person could do that by having sex eight times."

"Not the Surrys. Some of the things Nana told me, late in her life, say otherwise. And of course, he was so much older than she was. I know that Alan had a problem with sex. And Boydie was obsessed with it. And Enid. God. I can remember her saying to me one time, 'What's the most important thing about sex for you?' I answered, 'I'm not sure what you mean by sex, but I like the cuddling and the loving.'

"'Oh, bullshit,' she said. 'Not me.'"

"She was saying that she liked to screw?"

She wrinkled her nose. "I guess so. And Daphne, she was an enigma. Nobody ever knew what Daphne was thinking. She'd say the most dreadful things, always trying to shock people. And how much of it was real and how much show, I honestly don't know.

"You know, it's odd," she continued as another thought struck her. "In another way, my father was an extremely proper man. The day he went to the hospital—he died four or five hours later—he said to your grandmother, 'I'll tell you one thing, Jessie, I've never looked at another woman since the day I met you.'

"The trouble was, that was the only really wonderful thing she had to remember from their marriage. He had the disease of jealousy, and it ruined all our lives. He was jealous of his own son Alan, and by the time he was 15, Alan left home, changed his name, and didn't use his real name again to the day he died.

"He was cruel, my father. Alan was ill and so delicate as a child that Mum gave him more attention than she did the rest of us. He was her first-born, after all. But it made my father insanely jeal-ous—of his own son! Can you imagine that?

"I remember when I first got married, your father and I moved down to Camrose, and I had the twins and he'd be away all week. Then he'd come home weekends and disappear playing golf all weekend. So I didn't see him, period. Very selfish. I remember Mom came down one weekend on the bus. Nobody came to meet her, but she knew where we lived in this little town—it wasn't hard to find, I guess. And so the moment she got in the door she said, 'Where's Hartley?'

"'Oh, he's out at the golf club,' I said. 'He plays golf all week-end. I think he's got a woman out there.'

"She jumped on me, and said, 'I never want to hear you talk that way again. Your father ruined my life and all you kids' lives with his jealousy, and now you're starting. It's something you've got to fight.'

"She was odd that way. She defended your father against me every time if he and I were arguing, and he never had a clue she did that."

"That's sort of strange," I said. "You're talking about the person who went out of her way to tell me, when I was about 12, that my father hadn't wanted me to be born."

My mother shrugged. "He didn't," she said. "He didn't want any more children. I was the one who wanted another baby. One reason he didn't want another child was that he was just building the house you grew up in, and that's all he could think about. He'd begun by digging the basement—he had just enough money to do the basement. Then he'd go off to the bank, and get them to loan him 50 dollars, and he'd build something more, pay it off, and go back to the bank for another loan. That whole house was built that way, in bits and pieces. He'd hire a carpenter who'd show him how to put a window in, and then he'd fire the carpenter and put all the other windows in himself. He did the same thing with the doorjambs, and everything else. Your father could figure out almost anything once he put his mind to it.

"But from his point of view it was a bad time to be thinking of having children. It was the middle of the war, and people still didn't know what was going to happen, the house was unfinished, and he just didn't think it was wise to have another child in those circumstances. I pointed out to him I really hadn't gotten pregnant by myself, but that didn't matter to him. He was upset about it for a long time, but really, he got over it once you were born. So your grandmother made more of it than was there. Toward the end of her life, she had nothing to do but think about things that had gone wrong, and I guess this grew into a significance it didn't really have, along with a lot of other things. But so many times she'd take Hartley's part when he and I were fighting, and even though I'd be furious with her, she'd say her piece. 'Maybe you want to have an unhappy home like the one your father made for us,' she'd say. 'Well, jealousy is the best way to get that.'

"So I forced myself not to be jealous. I simply refused to allow myself to feel it. But it was hard. Your grandmother understood that. 'You know he's a travelling salesman,' she'd say, 'and he's going to be away all the time. Are you going to be imagining all the things he's going to do, like your father did every time I left the house?'"

"I've wondered that about Dad myself, him being a travelling salesman," I said.

She shrugged. "I don't think so. But it was true that he found being around all of us hard to take."

"I remember that when he went into business, he went down there all the time at night. He didn't seem to have a lot of heart for family life."

"Your father didn't have much of a heart, period," she said. Then, as if she'd realized that it wasn't that simple, she added, "You know, he couldn't hold you when you were throwing up or sick, but if you threw up on the floor, he could clean that up, and he often did, cheerfully. From the day I had that breast removed, he's never touched me there. If his arm touches me there during the night, he flinches, even now. Imagine the effect that has had.

"One of the wonderful moments in my secret relationship was when he came to Prince George. He said he was making chance visits here and there, but the truth was that he'd come to see me. Anyway, the first thing he said to me when we were alone was, 'Let me see it.'

"And he ran his hand over the scar, the way he had when I was in Vancouver for the radiation treatments. 'Ah well,' he said. 'Not too bad at all. They did quite a credible job. You'll be fine.' He was running his hands back and forth over the scar while he said all this. He wasn't revolted at all. So, there you are."

"There I am," I repeated. "I didn't know any of this."

She gave a short, curiously bitter laugh. "Now you know."

I shut off the tape recorder so we could go off the record. "What aren't you telling me?" I said.

She smiled. "Use your imagination. You're supposed to be good at that."

"Do you know if he's still alive?"

"I don't," she admitted. "Old age takes even those kinds of things from you. I always used to know where he was." She named a family friend who'd been one of his business associates. "Once he said to me, 'I don't know what you did to that man. I've travelled all over the world with him and he never looked at anyone before. What did you do to him?' I gave him my best blue-eyed smile and said, 'What are you talking about?' Neither of us ever admitted to anyone that there was anything between us, but he knew."

"Who else knew?"

"No one, really. It was my secret. Or, ours, rather, because he never told anyone either, as far as I know. I think your sisters may suspect something of it, but we've never talked about it."

She fell silent, and I kept a respectful distance from it, not wanting to disturb her reverie. After a moment, she looked up.

"You know that your father found his letters to me, don't you?"

"I didn't know there *were* letters," I admitted.

"There were quite a few. When your father found them, he phoned my man's wife in a fury and said—I don't know what he said to her. When I talked to my man a few months later in Vancouver, he sat me down and said, 'God, now what have you done? I told you to destroy those letters, but somehow I knew you weren't going to, and now, look what's happened. What did you tell Hartley?'

"'I said that you were just helping me through the cancer, which was true. I said that you encouraged me—which was more than he was capable of. I guess I lost my temper when I said that. I told Hartley that you actually cared about me, and not just about business. I told him that you saved my life. That's what I told Hartley.'"

"'Did he buy it?' he wanted to know. 'I really don't know,' I said. 'Well, I told my wife more or less the same. She was a little upset at first, but she got over it.'

"The truth was that he did save my life. But it could have been so much more. Maybe if we'd lived closer it wouldn't have ended the way it did, I don't know. But anyway, that's how it goes. As I said, he's the reason I've been able to cope with life the way I have. You never lose something like that, even if you . . ."

Her voice trailed off into a suddenly rich silence. It wasn't one I was going to tamper with, because I could see that she was back in that moment of decision, savouring it.

"I think," she continued, "that there are special things in the world that you don't go out looking for. They happen, they're there, they're a fact of life. If you experience them, you're lucky."

"You shouldn't feel guilty about this," I said. "He was a good man, and I think you're right: He did save your life."

"We didn't allow what was between us to hurt anybody. I mean, we didn't talk only about ourselves. We talked about our kids and what we hoped for them. He was concerned because his wife's parents were going to simply give everything to his son, and he didn't want that. He wanted his son to earn things. He said, 'My parents didn't put a silver spoon in my mouth. They told me to go out and earn what I wanted. So I won't allow them to do that to my son.' The last time I heard from him the son was the president of some big organization in the United States, I forget the name of it.

"When I think about him even now," she said, "I feel nice. I feel nice inside. I don't know whether that's right or not. Maybe that's not the right description, either, eh? But somehow there was never anything wrong about it. It didn't hurt anybody. Brian? It didn't hurt anybody."

I reached over and touched her hand. "No, it didn't hurt anyone."

Burial Plot

ABOUT A YEAR AFTER that conversation, my maternal
cousin Brian Manson and I scattered the ashes of my
mother's brother Ronald Surry—our common uncle—
on the grounds of Canada's Royal Military College in Kingston,
Ontario. He'd died ten years before, during a dreary end-of-winter
snowstorm in Penticton, British Columbia, in a basement apartment my mother owned, and was letting him live in, rent free.

Ronald had spent most of his adult life as a country gentleman in
rural Sussex, England, living in a stone house built in the sixteenth
century, raising pigs and drinking tanker-trucks of Merrydown
Apple Wine. He'd crash-landed in Penticton in 1982 after his

long-suffering wife of 35 years threw him out for being overbearing, miserable, and unhappy.

During World War II, he'd been a courageous army intelligence major in the Canadian army, a man who'd earned his commission defusing unexploded German bombs in London during the Blitz. My first meeting with him was in 1962, when I showed up on his doorstep as a terrified teenager trying to pretend I was a world traveller. He was middle-aged by then, and to my eyes, urbane and articulate. But even I could tell he was beginning to descend into an eccentricity that prominently featured a misanthropic agoraphobia and something akin to xenophobia without the racial or ethnic overtones: to him, everyone but his wife was a stranger, including, prior to his first evening drink, me. Years later, his wife hinted that he had seen things during the war—including a freshly liberated Nazi death camp—that no normal human being could witness and not be changed by.

Ronald died of a stomach ulcer hemorrhage. Given that stomach ulcers are a long-standing response to stress in my extended family and that the emergency procedures for preventing fatalities are familiar to us all, it is fair to say that Ronald chose to die when and as he did, if not precisely to commit suicide. He'd lived 71 years, smoked too much for at least 50 of them, and had gone to sleep

loaded most nights over the last 40. Still, aside from the ulcer, he was in relatively sound health when the Reaper arrived on the doorstep.

In the years he lived in Penticton, Ronald didn't make things easy for himself. Aside from nearly causing my parents to divorce, he was the more or less official Family Dragon—earning the title by frightening his grand- and great-grandnephews and -nieces with his imperious manner and his insistence on strict British formality—and, alternately and without any consistency, by offending the adults in the family sturdy enough to make duty visits, offering them drinks at ten in the morning, lecturing them on their inadequacies as British Subjects and if not that, then their inept impersonations of civilized beings. By the time he died, the family that had embraced him warmly on his return from England had more or less stopped coming around, and he was a man who'd managed to alienate everyone who'd ever cared about him. Or, almost everyone.

I was the first family member summonsed after my mother discovered his corpse. This was because I was the only one in the family—herself included—who still enjoyed Ronald's prickly company. I got myself to Penticton as she knew I would, and my mother and I sat down across the kitchen table and eyed each other solemnly.

"He said he didn't want a funeral," she said. "What do you think?"

"I heard all that nonsense, too," I said. "But you know, he was good to me when I was young. I owe him an acknowledgment of that. And he had a life once, quite a good and decent one. Maybe he gave up on the world, but you and I haven't."

Her quick smile told me she agreed. "Yes," she said, turning to gaze out the window at a flock of tiny quail rooting through the still-frozen ground beneath her bird feeder. "I don't think we ought to let him get away with this. To hell with him and his lousy attitude. Let's hold a memorial service."

Over the next 48 hours, my mother and I, with a cheerfulness that felt only a little perverse, organized a memorial service. We rented a space in one of Penticton's many non-denominational funeral chapels, and she issued no-option summonses to the family. Most of them showed up, too. So did Ronald's two estranged sons, one of whom flew in from Toronto, the other from Edmonton. Also at the service, unexpectedly, was a sprinkling of a dozen or so elderly women. These women were bridge players, and they'd made up Ronald's social circle during his last years. Before we went in, they had nice things to say about his skills as a bridge player, and alluded, discreetly, to his cultured personality without feeling the need to translate "cultured" as "difficult."

As I watched my family, which temporarily included Ronald's frozen-faced sons, file into the chapel, it occurred to me that my mother's motives for holding this service might be more complicated than they appeared.

This was our first family funeral. Remarkably, not a single blood relative had died on my parents' turf since they were married in 1936. Everyone in their immediate genetic line was alive: their children were, their grandchildren and great-grandchildren were— everyone, including spouses, stepchildren, and the numerous ex- spouses. *Everyone*. And despite her lifelong dislike of ceremonies and speech making, my mother, I think, had decided that sending on her miscreant brother this way would be a useful training exer- cise for the inevitable deaths to come, including her own and my father's.

The service began with a roll of mumbo-jumbo by the funeral director, who couldn't quite get a bead on Ronald's name and so referred to him as "the deceased." When he'd deposited enough vague comforts and inaccurate platitudes to convince himself that he'd adequately exercised his professional training and earned his fee, I got up and delivered the eulogy. I'd noticed during the funeral director's barrage of platitudes that I would be delivering to an audience that wasn't having any trouble keeping their eyes dry about the bereavement just suffered. To hell with them, too.

I began with Ronald's generosity when I appeared on his doorstep in 1962. I described how he and his wife Joan offered me the best things about a culture older and deeper than mine, and how they'd convinced me, both by example and some not-so-subtle cajoling, to respect and then enjoy its alien rhythms and formalities. They gave me books to read, music to listen to, French wine to drink and I proceeded to steal six months from their lives while they gave me an education northern British Columbia couldn't.

My eulogy of Ronald Surry praised the patience and forbearance he'd shown me, the gentleness of his pedagogy, and as I blathered on I saw my mother nod approvingly at the startled expressions on the faces of my audience as they realized that I'd known a man they knew nothing about.

There were some things I didn't talk about. His lousy behaviour toward his three children—two sons abandoned in Canada as infants; the third, the British-born daughter, driven away permanently before she got out of her teens—wasn't suitable eulogy material, nor were his two marriages to more-than-decent women he treated badly. At the time I knew next to nothing about his military career because he'd been reluctant to talk about the war. What little he had told me was spectacularly unsuitable for a eulogy, despite having held me spellbound as an 18-year-old. Like the other Surrys of his generation, Ronald enjoyed the give-and-take of conversation, but he couldn't resist the impulse to shock and appall. His explicit descriptions of women with irregular genital configurations and strange orgasm-related vocalizations were the sort of thing that tended to put people off balance at the best of times, let alone at funerals. Except for my mother, that was where the Surrys liked to hold others, even their loved ones—but I didn't talk about that, either.

I carried the eulogy out to a respectable length, ending it by offering the audience the coldest kind of truth about Ronald Surry I could muster: that he'd had a pretty interesting first half of a life, had wasted the other half, and that this was a bloody shame. From my mother's smile I knew I'd made a decent case for what she wanted the people there, family and strangers, to hear: that Ronald

Surry was like most human beings; worthy of love despite his flaws and his transgressions. I'd said goodbye to him for those kept from it by pride or injury, including my gentle English aunt whose love he'd squandered.

I shut up and sat down, the funeral director fired up some concluding platitudes, and everyone hustled out in the chilly March outdoors, including Ronald's sons, who didn't bother to go through his personal effects afterward for mementoes even though they were quite willing to accept their share of the modest estate he left behind. They preferred him as they had him, I guess, and it was hard to blame them.

When I left Penticton a few days later, my mother handed me a cardboard-wrapped package with Ronald's ashes inside. "You'll know what to do with these," she said. She clapped her hands together with a kind of finality that told me that for her, this was the end of it—and him.

*   *   *

I had no idea what to do with the ashes, and so for ten years, I did nothing. Then, over dinner in the spring of 1999 with my cousin Brian Manson, a retired schoolteacher and the family genealogist, I mentioned that I'd been sitting on Ronald Surry's ashes for a decade. He asked what I planned to do with them.

"I've been meaning to scatter them on the grounds at Royal Military College," I said, "but I've never quite gotten around to it. You know how it goes."

"Look," Brian said after a moment's thought. "I'll be out here again at the end of the summer. Why don't you and I drive to Kingston and do the ash-scattering together."

*   *   *

Despite the six months between plan formation and execution day, Brian and I arrive in Kingston without the slightest idea of how we're going to go about scattering the ashes. Winging it has been pretty much my lifelong method of getting things done, and having had ten years to formulate a plan for scattering Ronald's ashes hasn't changed that. The truth is that I damned well didn't want to make a plan, out of a superstition about death and human remains I was only dimly aware of having. The surprise is that my cousin, a man with a much more orderly mind than mine, thinks my Visual Flight Rules approach is just fine.

As we pull off the Macdonald-Cartier Freeway and drive south through the strip malls that ring downtown Kingston, I mention to him that what we're about to do is probably illegal. "This is military property we'll be littering," I say. "Or polluting."

"Why don't we just walk in and tell them what we'd like to do?" he suggests. "Maybe they'll give us a military escort and a 21-gun salute."

"And maybe they'll tie us up in red tape for five years, or throw us in their brig. Why take the risk?"

"Okay," he says. "We'll find someplace on the grounds where he'd likely have gone to think deep thoughts, and discreetly scatter him there. Incidentally, where is the old boy?"

I point to a rectangular package in the back seat of the car. "In there. I've never opened the package to see what kind of urn they put him in."

Brian reaches across the seat and pulls Ronald's remains into the front seat with him. "Hefty," he notes, tossing the package gently into the air.

* * *

Royal Military College sits on a peninsula of land between downtown Kingston and CFB Kingston, the only major urban army installation in the country. The college grounds are spacious, oddly free of ivy, and at their southern edge, they overlook the St. Lawrence River. The original fort on Point Frederick was built for the War of 1812, and in the 1840s, it was replaced by a moated Martello tower tall enough to sight incoming American warships. The now-moatless tower, which still stands, has seen its armaments rust awaiting the American invasion that has, well, never taken the form of a military foray across this stretch of water. Today the tower houses the college museum, and so is probably at the apex of its career usefulness. The college itself lies to the immediate north, with the complex of buildings where Ronald Surry received his training as an officer in 1942 set around a formal parade ground and playing field. The more contemporary educational adjuncts— mainly improved athletic facilities—lie farther north.

There is a guardhouse at the college gate, occupied by people wearing those silly military uniforms that don't tell you which branch of the service the wearer is in, but none of them seem interested in us. Pretty sure that this wouldn't be possible at West Point, we drive onto the college grounds unsupervised. We could be on the grounds of any college in the country except that here and there are morsels of military sculpture: an American Sherman tank, a second tank that appears to be a British Centurion, an American Sabre Jet, an authentically Canadian CF-100, along with a half-dozen obsolete artillery pieces I can't identify.

I find myself resorting to the Visual Flight Rules strategy I've always used in unfamiliar territory: I go until someone or something stops me, or I run out of interesting new things to look at. Since no one seems interested in stopping me and all the roads are open, I simply drive in the general direction of Lake Ontario, thinking that this will provide the picturesque and hopefully deserted spot where we can scatter the ashes and not get arrested. The roads run out pretty well where we want to be, at the edge of the college's original square where the oldest buildings cluster around a parade ground, about 200 metres from the lake and the Martello tower.

I stop the car and wonder aloud where we ought to park, noting that I've seen neither parking lots for visitors nor any NO PARKING signs.

"Why don't we just park wherever we want?" Brian says. "If they think we're threatening national security, they can shoot us."

I'm still thinking about whether they'll shoot us while I park next to the parade square. I shut off the car motor, then reach into the back seat for the carton containing Ronald's ashes and pull it into my lap, where I examine it closely for the first time. The cardboard package is sealed with reinforcing tape, and it isn't going to give up its contents easily. I fumble with the tape, eventually using the car key to separate the overlapping strips, and pull out a brick-coloured plastic cylinder. The weight of the package led me to expect a pottery urn, but this container is as disposable as its contents and a lot less biodegradable. On an impulse, I flip open the lid, careful to hold the cylinder level so the ashes don't spill inside the car. That's not a problem, because the ashes are inside a plastic bag.

"I guess we should look around, eh?" Brian says, sounding as tentative as I'm feeling. "Looks like a cafeteria in that building. Coffee, or something?"

We get out of the car and walk toward the building. I have the cylinder in my hands, which is a little dumb given that we're trying not to attract attention. I return to the car, pull my leather bookbag from the back seat and push the cylinder inside it, which is big enough that I can't quite close the zipper, and really does look like a bomb.

Brian spots a sign that tells us that a restaurant and store are located in the basement of the building we've parked beside, and moments later, we find ourselves in what would have been a cafeteria in our student days, and a canteen in Ronald's. The "store"— off to one side of the cafeteria—is a wholly contemporary touch, offering a variety of Royal Military College gear to the cadets and apparently to us, the general public. Obliged by the shop/op, we each buy a souvenir sweatshirt and then wander over to the cafeteria to purchase coffee in disposable cups. The coffee tastes like it was made while Ronald was a cadet here.

We sit down at one of the tables to drink it anyway, but we're still unable to formulate any sort of plan for scattering the ashes. What now prevents the planning, I think, is a shared picture we have in our heads of how the scattering of ashes *ought* to go: sombre music in the background, the two of us silhouetted against the sky releasing the ashes into the wind in a single motion so that the soul of Ronald Surry streams into The Vast Embracing Beyond with a graceful and cinematic flourish.

When we leave the cafeteria and walk to Point Frederick and the Martello tower to commit the real-world deed of scattering the ashes, there is, of course, no orchestra, no Steadicam with which to build the dramatic panorama we've got in our heads. There's just a landscape of stone and berms of green grass, with the chilly wind off the lake etching the silence. The expected poetry of the act is further curtailed because we're not even going to be able to silhouette ourselves against the sky. That would make us visible to a whole lot of order-obsessed people who will find our ash-scattering messy, unmilitary, and possibly unlawful.

Ronald's ashes have a similarly unpoetic character. The plastic seal on the bag won't open, and I have to rip a hole through its side with my car key. Then, there is far too much ash for a single scattering flourish, and worse, the ash has uncooperative properties. When

I make the first pass, turning my body in a circle with the opened container and bag held at shoulder level, most of the ash that does come out falls from the bag in a lump the consistency of wet concrete, while the rest atomizes in the air, covering us both with white dust.

Brian sensibly moves a safe distance off after the dusting, and begins to fiddle altogether too diligently with his camera, which is fully automatic and doesn't need any fiddling. I make a second pass across the grass with the ashes, this time with the container held below my knees. This produces less dust, but results in a trail of white across the grass that looks like I'm trying to use Ronald's ashes to line a baseball diamond. At the end of the pass the ashes that remain spill from the container, plastic bag included, and that forces me to a choice of abandoning the last vestiges of my mother's brother as they lie or shaking them—him—out onto the grass in a heap. I choose the latter, and am about to give the heap a scattering kick then I remember what—who—it is I'll be kicking. I pick up a handful and try to toss it—poetically—into the air in the direction of the Martello tower—and dust myself a second time.

As we retreat to the car, Brian voices the question I had about the ashes. "I wonder," he says, "if they have different-sized containers for different-sized people?"

"You noticed that the container was full."

"Yes," he says. "It was *perfectly* full. Did Ronald's ashes just happen to fill it exactly?" He leaves a pregnant pause in case I don't get it. I do, but say nothing, not quite wanting to admit to myself how alike our minds work. "Did they," he continues, "perhaps top his container up with someone else's ashes? Or did some of Ronald end up as fill in the container of some little old lady who'd weighed 90 pounds?"

I nod in agreement, but say nothing. There's a metaphor here, but I can't decide whether it reveals the essentials of Ronald Surry's life, or all of our lives. But on the way back to the car, passing the otherwise unremarkable windows of Fort Haldeman, one of the principal cadet residences and likely the building Ronald lived in during his tenure, I uncover a metaphor that actually does capture something of Ronald. I count 14 different steam irons in the different windows of the cadets' rooms, each one with the ironing surfaces facing the square. This is the most telling detail we've encountered, and the only one that separates this place from the grounds of a junior college or a mental hospital. The irons are an eloquent testimony to the orderliness of military life, something Ronald once told me he'd missed from the moment he resigned his commission.

While I count the irons in the windows a second time—wanting to secure their statistical reality—a disturbing detail of Ronald's death resurfaces. When my mother discovered his body, he was lying on his side on the bedroom floor, nude and curled into the fetal position, with his head pillowed on three carefully folded towels. His blood-soaked pajamas were beside him in a similarly ordered stack. There were signs around the apartment that he'd begun a cleanup of the blood he'd vomited, but with time running out, he'd had to choose between his need for orderliness and the knowledge that it would be my mother who would find him. His choice had been true to character, and now, all these years after his death, I realize that he'd had no time to iron either the pajamas or the towels. That must, as the world faded for the last time, have seemed life's final affront.

*   *   *

The cardboard package Ronald Surry's ashes rested in for ten years was still in the back seat of my car weeks later because I couldn't quite bring myself to throw it away. But eventually I got over that, and, except for the Omega Seamaster wristwatch he'd worn on

D-Day in 1944, and which I kept as a souvenir when neither of his sons wanted it, the last worldly traces of Ronald Surry were stuffed into a black plastic bag and taken away with the weekly garbage pickup. The Omega doesn't keep very accurate time, but the wristband is elegant, and it reminds me, whenever I put it on, of Ronald Surry's self-inflicted unhappiness, and how I *shouldn't* live my life.

Chess Game

MY FATHER was a chess player. He wasn't a very good one, but he understood what the game was about, and he challenged everyone to play him. Most of his grandchildren learned the game from him, and were drubbed mercilessly until one by one, they learned enough to play up to his level. My brother rarely played him even though he could defeat him easily, and after a while, I understood why. For either of *us* to lose to him was different than when the kids did: if he beat us, we were dopes. When we beat him, it was luck, and he'd get us next time—which was always sooner than either of us wanted.

I wasn't a serious chess player, but I won most of the games I played with him because it just plain cost too much to lose. Our games were deadly serious affairs: chess-matches-in-lieu-of-fights, with both of us channelling our mutual aggression into every match we played.

But once I'd done the 40 questions with my mother, I felt obliged to get my father's side. So the next time I was in Penticton I accepted the customary challenge of a chess match with him, beat him soundly, and then used the advantage to get him to sit down with the tape recorder while my mother was out doing her weekly volunteer stint at the hospital.

He and I had been in front of a tape recorder before. After our road trip in 1983, I talked him into dictating a short autobiography so he could tell the story of his life in his own words. He did, and with great relish. In the first version, he didn't mention that he had a wife and children. The story of his life, in his mind, had been "How I Succeeded in Business."

That may have been the story he wanted to tell, but it was a story I'd heard a thousand times, and I wanted more of him than his business philosophies, which everyone knew all about anyway. A couple of weeks after I sent him the first transcript, I drove up to Penticton and cornered him for the non-business details. I caught him in a good mood, and he gave up all sorts of anecdotes about his youth I hadn't gotten a hint of even on the road trip. He hadn't, it seems, always been the dour business-focused tyrant I knew.

He was pleased to have the little book I printed up 50 copies of, despite its off-topic anecdotes, and for a couple of years after that, we almost got along, and I told myself he was finally able to see the value of my being a writer. But this was nearly 17 years on, and he was about to turn 93. He and my mother were at the melt-down stages of their long war, and I wasn't even pretending to be neutral. I suspect he agreed to the 40-questions taping only because I told him I'd made a tape with my mother, and he wanted to set the record straight. We argued over whether he could see the questions before I asked them, but I hung tough, saying that I hadn't shown them to her, and what I wanted was the same kind of spontaneity.

After more wrangling and grumbling on his part—and with the chess defeat—he complied with my terms. "Setting the record straight" was, for once, more important to him than having control. But he made it clear that he didn't like the conditions, and as a result we'd been sniping at one another for several hours when we finally sat down across the dining room table.

He gave me a hard look as I pressed the record button. "Okay, smart guy," he said. "Shoot."

I began with some of the easy questions I'd asked my mother, hoping he'd get interested in them the way she had, and would let down his guard for the harder questions. No such luck. His defences were up, and he sloughed off the easy ones as if they were a waste of his time. His favourite colour?

"Green, but also blue, and red. Green represents freshness. Progress. Growing. New ideas. Nature. The other colours I like for contrast."

Favourite number? He frowned: "7 come 11."

"Did you ever play craps?"

"I never gamble," he said, glaring at me as if I should have known this. "It's a sucker's game. I don't play when the odds are stacked against me."

He admitted that he liked fresh, lean, sliced side pork, broiled. Cherries, raspberries, peaches, potatoes, pointing out that he froze the peaches he picked from the two small trees he'd planted in the front yard. Potatoes french-fried, but due to the high fat content of french fries, other methods were now employed: sliced and cooked with milk, hash browns. His lecturing tone let me know he thought the questions were frivolous.

I understood what was going on: he was trying to give me nothing but philosophy, and as few facts as he could, even if he had to lie. I knew, for instance, that he liked potatoes boiled, and not quite fully cooked. I was also waiting for—and dreading—the Barley Max lecture, which he was entertaining himself by selling to everyone who came near enough to be collared. The product was manufactured in the American Midwest, and along with it came a deluge of Republican-Christian fundamentalist propaganda that placed it in the zone of the colonic irrigation cleaner-than-thou crowd, as a kind of intestinal cleanser with political propaganda instead of the garden hose up the ass. Never a man with half-hearted opinions, my father proselytized Barley Max as a cure for *all* human ills, including the socialist tendencies that he regarded me as polluted with. Over the years he'd managed to bullyrag my brother and sisters into taking it—or pretending to—but I wasn't having any of it, and not just because it was foul-tasting. The reality was that I was being as childish about not taking it as he was about propagandizing it, and it had turned into a particularly silly episode in our long-standing contest of wills. I made a point of telling anyone who would listen—in his hearing range—that it tasted like something only cows would enjoy, and that I couldn't see much advantage in a product that required me to have a second stomach to digest it properly.

Now I was about to pay for being a smartass. Raising the question of food favourites gave him the opening to launch into a ten-minute infomercial about the virtues of Barley Max. I sat through it without complaint because I wanted the interview, and as always with him, I had to pay his price. He even kept his eyes on the tape recorder so I couldn't turn it off. If there was going to be a record, this was what he wanted on it.

On the interview crawled; guarded answers to trivial questions. Favourite trees: cherries because they bear fruit, Colorado blue spruce, of which he had two in his yard, pruned so heavily they were wider than they were tall. Favourite fish: halibut (the first thing we agreed on). Favourite music, country: Favourite song: "Just a

Closer Walk with Thee," which he said he wanted played at his funeral in waltz time so it wouldn't be so depressing.

When I asked him which scents brought him pleasure, he laughed for the first time.

"Ah," he said. "All good scents. But the scent of cooking food most. Also, 'cents' bring 'dollars,' and dollars bring many good things, ha, ha."

I gave up on the preliminaries, cut several questions I knew he wouldn't give me a straight answer to, and got to the first serious question, realizing as I read it out that it was loaded. "What thing or person in your life has brought you the greatest pleasure?"

He stopped looking bored, and glared at me. "Business success has given me the greatest pleasure," he said. "But I also take pleasure in all my family. I have no favourites."

I went for the bait, thinking that I could avoid another philosophy lecture with a minor confrontation. "Why is it important that you have chosen no favourites?"

I'd misread him. To him, this wasn't a hook but a flashing blade. He was going for revenge.

"Well," he said, "maybe I do have some favourites. I worked and developed Ron for 35 years. And although we've had our ups and downs and disagreements and mistakes, we persevered and established a successful business. It took much time and effort, and it is now family oriented. I want it to continue to grow and serve the interests of the family. Jason [Ron's eldest son] gives me much promise and confidence. I am thrilled by his actions and progress."

Was he trying to put the knife into me here, or was he offering, in the wake of having given the voting shares in his company to Ron, a backhanded explanation? And what was I supposed to do with it? Why *shouldn't* he prefer my brother, who'd looked up to him, agreed with him, worked with him most of his life, lived with the endless browbeatings. I'd never walked across a street to co-operate with him. Was I supposed to win his respect by fighting with him over every absurd ego-point? The crazy thing was that I *had* won his respect. But was he then supposed to trust me with his beloved assets? I found myself, suddenly and surprisingly, inside his head: *No Bloody Way.*

I also couldn't help admiring his tactical skills. He'd turned this one on me, and he'd done it accurately. I'd come into the interview with an agenda of my own, and he wasn't having any of it. He didn't trust me any more than I trusted him, and he was right not to. I needed a break to rethink what I was doing. I clicked off the tape recorder and asked him if he wanted a cup of tea.

"Sure," he said, warily. "Why not?"

I made the tea and we drank it, white and with lots of sugar, and he launched into another infomercial about why Barley Max was a Great Product, and why I ought to be taking it. Barley Max wasn't a business to him. He was selling the stuff for less than he paid for it: $32 for a quart container he'd paid $35 US to buy wholesale. It was, he explained when I'd pointed this out to him, his idea of public service, improving community and family health. I reached over and pushed the record button on the recorder.

"What physical activities have brought you the most pleasure?"

His eyes narrowed, and I thought he was about to ask me why I was so concerned about pleasure. "Curling, and walking. That's about all I can do these days. Maybe digging in the garden a little."

"What activities gave you pleasure when you were, say, 30 years old?"

"Oh, hell," he said, "that was a long time ago. But I loved my job selling and I was good at it."

I settled back in my chair, ready to wait this one out while he gave me the philosophy part of it. But that's all he wanted to say, so I asked him what mental activity now brought him the greatest satisfaction.

"Chess," he said. "It's all logic, no luck or chances. As You Think, So Shall You Be. The Power of your Reason will be the Reality of Tomorrow. Chess is true to facts, just like Nature and Life are."

I resisted—just barely—asking him why I usually beat him at chess. But I took the high road on that, shuffled my question sheet for a moment and asked, "Why are we alive?"

For a moment, his guard went down, but only for a moment. He rolled his tongue around his mouth, took a sip of tea. "Because" he said, pushing the word over its two syllables while he tested his answer for flaws, "God created Adam and Eve, put them in the Garden of Eden with everything they needed and told them to Go Forth and Multiply. Now we have two billion Chinamen and a 14-million increase every year."

"There's just over a billion people in China right now," I said, "but I think the world population is increasing at a rate closer than 140 million a year than 14. But never mind that. Let's try the question in another way: What do you think the purpose of human life is?"

"We have the same Purpose as All Other Things that Live," he said, keeping the same unctuous tone. "To Grow and Reproduce in This World. We are part of a Total Scheme, following our Instincts as Life Unfolds, like All Other Species."

"I guess what I'm asking is whether you think life has some 'higher' purpose we've been put on the earth to pursue."

"'Do Unto Others As You Would Have Them Do Unto You' satisfies me," he said. "Everyone is different and has to do his own thing. It's hard to change people. They have to be Self-motivated and Pliant and Intelligent to Change. It is a slow progress at best. Some of us are Lucky. I inherited a lot of Good Qualities from my mother, God bless her."

I thought about asking him if he agreed that cows should give milk, but held my tongue. "Does God exist?" I asked.

"Yes," he said, "sure."

The swift flatness of his answer was a small surprise, given that he hadn't seen the inside of a church in 40 years. It hadn't been atheism so much as being otherwise engaged: hard to make a buck out of believing.

"In what form, and for what purpose, does God exist, then," I said. "Is he a guy in a white robe sitting at a boardroom table?"

"I don't know," he said. "I believe the subject to be Beyond my Comprehension."

I thought he was done, but he shifted in the chair and delivered a small triumph of his native common sense over his philosophy. "Most people in the world are hypocrites and violent people and many of the problems we have stem from organized religion. Although it sometimes moves things to the better, it is also exploited by the Strong to control the Weak."

"Then what's the most important thing in life?"

"Good Health," he answered, again without hesitating. "Without it you have nothing. That's why I Promote and Sell Barley Max."

"What would you have said if I'd asked you this question 25 years ago?"

He thought about that for a moment before answering. "You could," he said, slowly, "have asked me a lot of questions when I was at different ages and you'd have gotten different answers. Time plus Experience Equal Knowledge. The Things You Do and the Experience You Gain are Lessons You Never Forget, and when you discover something good that helps People Live a Better Life, you pass it on. Like Barley Max."

I laughed out loud at his refusal to give up control, even for a second, over what was clearly a game to him. I could ask my questions, but he was damned well going to answer his own questions. He smirked, as if he knew what I was thinking.

"Which person," I asked, "most influenced you in your life?"

His grin died. "My wife," he said.

"Okay. Nothing to add to that?"

"Nope. That's the answer."

"Which person had the most positive influence?"

Another two-word answer, this time delivered more slowly: "My wife." His expression signalled that he wasn't going to elaborate.

"Which person had the most negative influence?"

"My wife."

I should have seen this coming, but I didn't. "Okay," I said, trying to collect myself. "Do you want to leave that as it is for all your future grandchildren and great-grandchildren without explaining what it means? I have an inkling of what you mean by it, since I've been around it. Pretty well anyone who's lived with someone for 60 years might say something like this. I'd like you to explain *why* she's been a positive influence and how and where she's been a negative influence. We can leave it off the record if you want. But since it's my job in this family to find out what people really think, and to learn what goes on beneath the obvious surfaces, I'd appreciate it if you'd help me do my job here."

"Your wife is the one you see and live with every day," he said, carefully. "You are both dependent on each other. I had a brother whose domineering wife drove him senile. That was a lesson I've never forgotten. You've got to remember that I was born on a farm, and it had no future. Therefore I had to create an Independent Life for myself."

He let a long pause get longer, as if inviting me to weigh the accuracy of what he'd just said. Then he concluded, in lower case, "I've never been prepared to give up that independence."

"And the trouble was, Mum wouldn't give up hers, either? Fair enough," I said, trying not to show my surprise at his candidness. "Let's go back a little. Who or what was the main influence before you were, say, 21."

"My father. He was a tight, miserable man. My mother was lov-ing, kind-hearted, hard-working, compassionate, and generous. She had all those good qualities and she passed them on to me."

"Which of the two people had the bigger influence on you? The good person, or the bad person?"

The wall went back up. "The Good you Adopt," he said. "The Bad you Discard and Forget."

"Yes, I understand that," I said. "But you haven't forgotten the bad. What do you think made your father the way he was? Was it his character, or was it his experiences?"

He turned this over for a moment, decided it wasn't a set-up, and mulled it over some more. "I think," he said, "it was likely his experiences. He had a hard life, and money was always scarce. He was endeavouring to claw his way up and money was the necessary commodity to do that. Therefore, he became a slave to its produc-tion and preservation."

He was done, so I let it go. "How," I said, "would you describe your politics?"

He puffed up, quickly back inside his comfort zone. "Practical and Common Sense. I pick the party with the most Practical Pro-gram. Socialists and Trade Unions are taboo. If I had been Mul-roney or Trudeau I could have taught Canadians how to Pay As They Go and that would have saved 43 billion a year on our taxes. There are No Free Lunches, in other words. That sort of sums up my politics."

He went on to mention several right-wing politicians he admired. It was almost a set piece for us, and there was no point in arguing it again. "When," I asked, "were you the most happy and fulfilled during your life?"

He looked at me hard. "Since I Accept Life as It is Presented, and I Adapt, I am Always Fulfilled. But I was most Happy and Fulfilled when I was Working and Creating a Business Empire Successfully. That still makes me the most Happy and Fulfilled I could be, and I'm still at it."

"In the photos from the old days, you look pretty happy. Were you? Would you say that some kinds of happiness don't offer people much of a future, and that one therefore must make choices based on what kind of future is in the offing?"

He looked for the trap, found it, and sidestepped it. "You Do Your Best and Work on the Problems at Hand. Only then can you pass on to Greater Achievements. A man who Adapts and seems Happy and Gregarious is much more likely to be Successful. People like Happy People, and Success Follows from that Appearance."

He thought about this for a moment, then added, "On the other hand, I have always been Happy and Satisfied. My philosophy is that you Accept Life and Work at it."

I decided to press him a little. "If that was true, wouldn't you'd still be on the farm? If someone is pushing your face into the dirt the way your father did, can you really be happy and satisfied? Aren't there some things a man *can't* work at?"

"Well, you Make the Best of Present Circumstances, and you can Work Hard and Look for Something Better."

Another pat answer. I looked down at my sheet. The next question wasn't one he was going to entertain for a moment, but I asked it anyway. "If you were to go home, in the spiritual sense, where would it be to?"

"The Grave," he said.

"I don't understand what you mean by this," I said. "Are you saying that because you're the last of your generation, or is there something I'm missing? You've always looked pretty much at home wherever you were, and since you still do, saying that being dead is your spiritual home doesn't add up. I've always thought your 'spiritual home' was down at the plant working on some piece of machinery that wasn't quite working right but which you were convinced you could fix—the compressor on one of the freezer trucks, for instance. That's what I see when I think of you at the height of your powers, and at the pinnacle of your happiness. Try to look at this question in that sort of light, and see if you can find the best place in your world in that way."

He gave me a look that told me he was trying to figure out if I was setting him up again. "As I told you," he said, carefully, and momentarily without any upper case, "I was happiest Building my Empire. I was a Builder. For me, that all came crashing down when my two heirs took off on me."

There was a long silence as I let this ancient piece of family mayhem rest in front of us both. For sure, I had no answer, at least not one he'd accept. I looked up and into his eyes for a long moment. To anyone watching, we would have looked like a couple of dogs stiff-legging around one another, each one waiting for the provocation that would commence the scrap.

Time to change my tack. "Where is the most beautiful place in the world?"

"My Home."

A trick answer? "I don't want anyone to be confused by this. You're talking about where we are right now: 177 Westview Drive, right?"

"Home is Wherever I Live."

I thought about this for a moment, and realized it was more accurate than he intended, and more bitter. He couldn't win his battle with his wife, he hadn't won his battle to control his sons, so screw you all if you won't do what I tell you to, I'm still on top, and I'm still me. If life had defeated this man in any profound way, here it was. And here *he* was, in his nineties, still mortally pissed off about it. Probably he'd always be.

"What things from the past do you miss most?"

"I miss my youth and energy and outlook," he said, with real regret in his voice.

"Who from the past do you miss the most?"

"My old pal, Len Elliott. I miss playing horseshoes with him."

This was bullshit, because Len beat him at horseshoes most of the time, and my father disliked him for it. But it wasn't worth an argument.

"Who from before you moved to Penticton do you miss most?"

He pondered this for a moment. "I chummed mostly with Wally West and Al Bowie back in Prince George, but both of them were dependent on their wives for their success and when the wives died, they both fell apart. So I don't miss them much."

"What thing from before you moved to Penticton do you miss most?"

"The Business and its Challenges," he said, quickly. "I still have dreams about the daily problems I had to solve there. I miss that. Funny, eh?"

I wondered if I should admit to him that I too had similar dreams, but decided that he'd take it the wrong way. I consulted my list of questions, didn't find one that connected, and made up one.

"Which of your brothers and sisters do you miss most?"

"My sister Lucy was the last of them to go, but you know, we were not a close family. I attempted reconciliation many times with my brothers but their wives disrupted my efforts. So I don't miss any of them."

This was the third answer on this theme, and it made me realize how isolated he must feel, and how long that sense of isolation had dogged him—most of his adult life, actually. He was a man unwilling to truly partner with anyone on an equal basis, not with his wife, not with business associates, not with his sons. Nobody. All his life he'd insisted, then and still, on being that sole dog with its tail up.

But the curiosity here was that he'd constantly sought the company of people who refused to put their tails down. I found myself wondering how my brother maneuvered around this on a day-to-day basis, and then it came to me: Ron's tail could now be up because my father had convinced himself that he'd invented the tail. So to him, it was *his* tail my brother was wagging.

"What is the most surprising thing anyone has ever done to—or for—you?"

"Ron, when he came into my office and said, 'I'm leaving.' The bottom dropped out of my world. But I try never to be surprised. I Take Life as it Presents Itself and Roll with the Punches."

I ignored this return of upper case, and moved on. "What is the most daring thing you've ever done?"

This was an easy one, and I got the answer I was expecting. "Going into business," he said.

"Can you talk about that a little? Why was going into business when you were in your forties more daring than, say, leaving the farm when you were 14 years old, or driving across that Edmonton bridge along the centreline at 75 miles an hour with cars coming both ways?"

He frowned, as if the question was idiotic. "By going into business I was giving up a good living, 19 years of seniority, a pension, and I was putting my home, my family, and my savings on the line for an unknown future."

His eyes momentarily clouded, as if he was remembering the uncertainty he'd felt then. Just for a moment, I caught the flavour of his fear, and it startled me. Then, as if sensing my empathy, he tried to hide his vulnerability in a string of clichés: "The Power," he intoned, "of Your Vision and the Determination to Make It Happen is the Reality of Tomorrow. You Don't Look Back Unless You Want it to Go In That Direction."

"What is courage?"

For a moment he was silent. Then he reached into his pack of philosophical slogans and came up with one: "What the Mind can Conceive and Believe with Courage and Determination, the Body can Achieve. No one can make you feel Inferior without your Consent."

He wasn't going to answer the question, so I asked him another. "Is your life a success?"

No hesitation. "Yes," he said. "Overwhelmingly so. Beyond my utmost ambitions and hopes."

I pressed another version of the same question at him, trying to get him beyond his platitudes. "What did you fail at that you think you should have achieved?"

He gave me a calculating look before he answered. "I didn't," he said slowly enough that I couldn't miss what he was implying, "always build my business on a business basis. You can't favour any-thing or anyone and build a successful business."

I could see that he was telling me something he didn't think I'd want to hear, but I couldn't quite see what it was. "Could you elaborate on what you mean by this?" I said. "I mean, you built a successful business. Are you saying you could have made it more successful? By doing what, exactly?"

"I mean that you have to build on merit, not on kin. Business is like chess. It's all logic. I built on kin and when my kin walked off I was old and vulnerable. The business collapsed and was picked up by others to Profit From and Enjoy."

There was an answer I could have given him: if he hadn't busted our balls all the time, and if he hadn't set us up to compete against one another for his approval, we might not have left. But that was for my brother to say if he wanted to, and he hadn't needed to. Or maybe he *had* said it, and I'd never heard about it. If I said it here, he might recognize just how casually and easily I'd walked away, and that would add humiliation to the existing injury. There was one more thing that I wasn't going to tell him about: that my brother and I had never forgiven one another for what happened, and that we hadn't been close since because of it. But hurting my father was one thing, giving him satisfaction was another.

I consulted my list. "Why did you succeed where your brothers and sisters didn't?"

"Simple," he said. "I had a vision of what I wanted to do with my life. That is vital to reaching your Full Potential, no matter what or who you are. Your Visions are the Reality of Tomorrow."

"Really?" I said. "Then can you tell me what constitutes a good life?"

"Good Health, Financial Independence, and a Loving Family, in that order."

He stopped to think that over, and added, "All three are necessary for a good life."

I read down my list of questions, decided to skip the several he was just going to sling more of this kind of bullshit at. I found one he couldn't bury. "Which gender is superior?" I asked. "And why?"

"Men are Superior. There has to be a Leader in All Things and Men were Created to Lead. A man naturally has all the Abilities and Opportunities to draw upon."

Okay, I thought to myself. This isn't worth arguing about even if I think he's dead wrong. I went to the next question on my list. "Other than yourself, which person in the world do you most admire? And why do you admire him?"

He brushed off my jab and landed his counterpunch. "Ron," he said. "I know he's had his problems, but he has worked at them and now he's Conquered his Shortcomings. And I must say, I've had a lot to do with it. The last three years he has blossomed into a Competent, Reliant, Confident CEO."

I considered asking him if the word "reliant" should be "reliable." But I'd gotten in the other crack, and he either hadn't noticed it or accepted its accuracy. It *was* true that he admired himself more than anyone else. Did I have a problem with that?

I asked another kind of question: "If you had it to do all over again, what things would you change?"

"Just one thing," he said, getting up from the table and walking stiffly into the kitchen, stretching his arms wide as if it might make the question go away. "And that's a secret."

I waited for him to go on, but he didn't. I didn't have a clue what his secret was, and I wasn't going to leave it hanging. "Okay," I said. "But off the record if you want, what's the secret? Someone in the family ought to know. If not me, then Ron. You don't want to go to your grave holding something like this over everyone's head. If you do, we'll all assume it has something to do with something we did. People are like that."

He poured himself a glass of water, and drank it down, clearly trying to decide whether to trust me. He bent over to put the glass in the dishwasher, straightened, and returned to the table. But he didn't sit down.

"Talking about this is against my principles," he said. "But all of my children have faced this and corrected it. I made some feeble attempts to do that but then I reneged and decided that it wasn't worth it. I wanted to continue Building My Empire. Your mother would have wanted half of the money, and that would have scuttled my ambitions. So I decided to Adapt and Tolerate."

He sat down, and leaned toward me as if he was about to impart a great truth. "You see," he said, "your mother is a Domineering Person, possessed of Moods that Flare and require Patience and Control and Acceptance and Forgiveness on my part. I have Developed all those Qualities in making my life as pleasant as possible under the circumstances. There. Now you have it. It's no longer a secret."

We were done. I already knew that he thought life was worth the trouble, and that he wouldn't be candid about any questions concerning sex. What he'd just told me wasn't so much a secret as the crappy sum total of the domestic war I'd been an intimate witness to most of my life. His sum total wasn't so different than my mother's: *sometimes there is no right thing to do, and it's just a mess.*

"One last question," I said. "And I really want to know the answer. Why do you enjoy cheating at cards so much?"

He didn't even blink. "I don't cheat," he said. "I just pretend that I do to get people's reactions."

Dying and Killing

MY SISTER Nina called me on the first day of December 2000, just after one in the afternoon: my mother had suffered a stroke, a major one. I was to come immediately.

"Ron is already on his way," she said. "Serena and I are leaving for the ferry in about an hour."

I made the distance calculations in my head: Ron was in Kamloops, 230 kilometres and three hours away. The twins would take longer. They'd have to make the hour-long drive from Parksville on the east coast of Vancouver Island to the ferry at Nanaimo, which would take them to Vancouver in about two more hours if the ferry lineup was short. Then another five hours by road to Penticton if the roads were clear. I was in Toronto, across the country, so it would take me at least a day to get there.

"How soon can you come?" I heard Nina say.

"Sometime tomorrow," I said. "If I'm lucky with the airlines, it'll be early in the day. If not—"

"I've got to go," she said. "Serena's here."

"I'll see you tomorrow," I said, then added, "Call me tonight when you get in."

I heard a click on the line, and I hung up, too. I'd felt no surprise when Nina told me what happened, just a surge of adrenalin. Now the adrenalin was swinging me into the darker realm of dread: I was not, despite my mother's attempts to prepare me, ready for this. She and I had talked about it in generalities; what could happen, what she wanted done when it did. My sisters had been given written instructions more than a year ago, and I had a copy of them somewhere in my desk. Two days ago she'd mentioned, almost in passing, twinges in her head, dizzy spells that didn't feel quite right. This had been the second call in a row where they'd come up.

"It's just a passing thing," she'd said. "Nothing to be really alarmed about."

She'd had several small strokes over the previous six years. The first had gotten her in a Penticton supermarket while she was shopping. She made her way to a bench near the cashier and sat down, hoping that it would fade and she'd be able to finish her errands. She spent half an hour humming to herself while she sorted through her purse, trying to convince anyone who noticed—and herself— that she was just fine, a happy old lady taking a break while she looked over her shopping list. That was when the second stroke hit her, this time a harder thump inside her brain that took out her sense of balance. She waited a few more minutes, teetering back and forth on the bench, still hoping it would pass: still, absurdly, hoping to get her shopping done. When it didn't pass, and she realized that she couldn't stand, she called over a clerk, and got him to phone my father.

The strokes were minor, but it was weeks before she could walk unaided, and she'd remained permanently shaky on her feet after that. Who knows how many more that she'd said nothing about had followed those first two? None? A dozen? I didn't know, and I'm pretty sure her doctor didn't know the exact total.

But she knew, and she wasn't one to kid herself about such things once she'd gotten a bead on them. She'd also known, from the first small strokes, what the eventual outcome was likely to be, and in the several months leading up to December the first, she'd laid down subtle hints for us to pick up. Beyond the set of written instructions, she'd made it clear she didn't want to talk directly about it. That wasn't her way. Instead, she laid down a carpet of subliminals that she hoped would become visible to us when the inevitable happened.

Mostly we ignored them, the way I did when we'd talked before. And so I was shocked by the reality of what was happening, but it was the shock of someone who knows a storm is approaching. You understand that rain and wind are on the way, but the rain, when it begins to fall, is cold anyway, and the chilly violence of the wind still takes your breath away.

Before I could process what I was feeling, a sliver of resentment elbowed its way in: this should have happened to my father. He was older, wasn't he? No, that wasn't quite it. After a lifetime of unproductive arguments and confrontations, nearly all unresolved and not likely to get resolved, I'd almost welcome *his* death, or at least be able to move on without difficulty, maybe with a sense of relief that our war was over. But for my mother's death I was woefully unprepared. As I wandered around the house in the moments after my sister's call, my emotions were running pretty much as they did while I was a small child, anxious that she was about to go out for the evening: What would become of me if she didn't come back?

I didn't talk about it with my brother and sisters, but in those first hours, each of us probably experienced something similar. Yes, we were grown adults, and competent ones, most of the time. But we were also the children she'd borne into the world and then nurtured, and for the next few weeks, those children would be closer to our collective and individual emotions than they had been in many years.

My mother had prepared me—more successfully—with a strict set of protocols for behaviour during a crisis: suppress your emotions, particularly the sentimental impulses, do what has to be done to get yourself and others through it, then deal with the aftermath on your own time. It had seen me through four marriage breakups, and dozens of accidents and other bits of mayhem. I'd seen my brother operate by this system when his domestic life had come apart and I knew he'd hold together here. I assumed that my sisters also would know how to handle themselves. We'd get through this, then, and on the terms our mother had set: there were to be no heroic measures by the doctors, we were to be there as comforts to her and as witnesses if the circumstances allowed for it. But we were to let her die, and we were to get on with our lives after she was gone.

We wouldn't be expecting much from my father. For at least a quarter century he'd been increasingly consumed by his phobia about death and illness, avoiding it with others well beyond the boundaries of social nicety, often walking away from conversations in which his elderly friends were enumerating their various maladies and the medical procedures they'd just had or were scheduled for—unless he could make a Barley Max pitch. He could make it to his own medical appointments, but only if my mother made a scene, and he didn't like funerals. Too much goddamned negativity for him.

"It's a good idea to stay away from hospitals," he'd say without a trace of humour. "People die in hospitals." Then he'd launch into the sales pitch for Barley Max. His phobia had become a family joke that was only a little dark: we joked to one another that he was so afraid of dying that he'd probably live forever.

The not-so-funny side of it was that he was little help in the face of incapacity or the other catastrophes life drops on everyone. He didn't respond when my siblings and I were in the glue except to offer the usual Rotary Club philosophies and platitudes. And he was now going to ignore or trivialize the death agony of the woman he'd lived with for 64 years.

But nothing, of course, is that black and white. One time, the motor of my Volkswagen blew up a few miles outside Penticton just after I'd broken up with my first wife. My son Jesse, just over two at the time, was with me, and I was, as usual in those days, broke. My father towed the car into town behind his Cadillac, and after we got a new motor for the little car, he said, "Why don't you fix the rust on this thing while you're here? May as well paint the damned thing while we're at it."

So that's what we did. The two of us spent most of four days pounding out dents, trowelling Bondo into the wheel-wells and along the rusted doors, and then power-sanding and wet/dry sanding the entire car. As we worked, my father piled on his Rotary Club homilies and talked about how I could remedy my character flaws. I dodged what I could, licked my wounds in silence when I couldn't, and tried not to let him see it bothered me. A week later I had a bright yellow mechanically sound car that got me through the next several years.

I was too stupid to acknowledge that we'd had fun working together, that I'd learned several useful skills or that when I returned to Vancouver I was more or less undamaged by his bullying. There was always that cost of doing business with him, but I despised business too much to accept even its practical transactions. My loss.

Within the family there was never much complaining about this particular flaw in my father's character, maybe because we knew that complaining wouldn't help. We rolled our eyeballs when he got going, my mother would snort in disgust, open the fridge and stare into it as if the remedy was in there somewhere. He was what he was, and we all understood, whenever his phobia about age and illness came up, that it was part of his survival strategy. But now, it meant that we were going to have to handle the end of our mother's life without much participation from him. So be it.

I was on a flight the next morning. Toronto to Calgary, Calgary to Kelowna. From there, I rented a car for the 60-kilometre drive to Penticton. I could have asked to be picked up, but having my own wheels was a long-standing precaution against being at the mercy of my father's provision. With the three-hour difference in the time zones, I was in Penticton by midafternoon, I think.

*   *   *

Let me clarify this "I think." In a mortal crisis, it is bad form to take field notes or take pictures, and thus I have to rely on memory, of which I possess, as noted earlier, the kind that stores by mental snapshots and slapstick, not with the high-resolution sequential stuff that some people are blessed with. Thus, I recall the first 90 seconds of the initial phone call and its aftermath. But the next picture is the light dusting of snow in the parking lot of the Penticton hospital. I *believe* that I drove directly to the hospital from Kelowna without stopping first at the house, but I'm not completely clear about that. One or both of my sisters *might* have been at the hospital when I arrived. I don't remember that, either. All I have is a dusting of fresh snow in the hospital parking lot, the chill in the air, and, wait a minute, that as I approached the hospital desk, I felt a surge of vertigo that nearly brought me to my knees. There was to be no slapstick for a few weeks, and very little laughter.

The next memory snapshot is from the doorway of my mother's hospital room. One of my sisters is probably in the room—again, I'm not sure, because only my mother is in the frame. Had I talked to anyone in the hallway? I don't recall. But there is a window behind the bed, with the drapes closed. I'm sure of that, and that the room is painted a pale blue instead of the expected institutional green, and that the bed is placed east/west. My mother is lying on her side, her back toward the wall. I recall a feeling of relief that she was in a private room. Someone must have gone over my father's head on that one, I thought. My brother's work, probably, or a courtesy granted to her for working at the hospital all those years as a volunteer. Had my father been involved, she'd have been in a ward to save the extra expense: private rooms cost money.

She seemed smaller. *Smaller than in life*, I remember thinking. She was lying on her left side, unmoving, staring at something near the bottom of the bed. I entered the room, not sure what to expect. Was she sleeping? Unconscious? Or was she there, inside her paralyzed body, fully aware?

The clinical description of what had happened inside her brain reads this way: *Major infarction by MCA (middle cerebral artery) stroke results in sensory loss and weakness that are most prominent in the part of the face and in the extremities opposite to the side of the brain where the stroke has occurred; such infarction causes as well a condition called aphasia—the loss of power of expression—although comprehension tends to remain reasonably well preserved.*

What I saw in those first minutes with her confirms that clinician's description: the right side of her face, first of all, was blank without being peaceful. Not empty, but rather, vacated, absent. Then she blinked, realizing that someone was in the room. She struggled to move her body so she could see who it was, and failed. I reached out, took her left hand in mine, and moved into her field of vision, kneeling at the side of the bed.

Half of her face animated: recognition, pleasure—in that order, and with a delay in the transition. She's there, I thought, but damaged, and thus slower. Then the "things have come to this" shrug/grimace that became, over the next days, my firmest conduit to her. It was not a gesture I'd ever seen her make before. It was, rather, a contorted summary of what the stroke had done to her. It was also strangely characteristic, and it was uncontestable evidence that she was there, her mind—or a part of her mind—intact. But what part, exactly?

Over the next several hours I was in and out of the room, and so were my brother and sisters—not quite buzzing around—but present. We easily agreed on the basics: she wasn't to be alone for the duration, particularly not during the night, and that meant we would take shifts attending her. Without thinking about why, I offered to take the midnight-to-6-a.m. stint. If I'd been paying attention, I would have left that to my brother, who was the only one of us who needed the private time with her. He had things to resolve, and I didn't. Instead, we stayed in our old roles: he handled the practical stuff, and I handled the intimacies.

Before I got there, one of my siblings had made a crucial mistake. It wasn't egregious, but it had penetrated the medical code in the worst possible way. The No Heroic Measures agreement was long settled between all of us, and countermanding my mother's wishes wasn't an issue, in any of our minds. She'd been clear that she wasn't interested in lingering on with profound physical and mental impairment. As she'd put it a dozen times with each of us, she'd had a long life, and that was enough. Like all the Surrys, death held no terror for her.

What we didn't know was that, by itself, "No Heroic Measures" can project a course of decline and death that is unspeakably cruel and painful to an otherwise healthy person who has suffered a major stroke. In essence, it condemns that person to a death by dehydration and/or starvation. The body will slowly deplete itself of fluids and nutrients, and depending on the health and body form of the "patient," up to 14 days can pass before fluid begins to collect in the lungs, and pneumonia sets in. Left untreated by antibiotics, another two to five days of drowning agony can ensue before death occurs. Until the pneumonia progresses, the victim of this barbarous procedure is fully conscious.

Given my mother's careful preparations, I'm pretty certain that she had a tacit agreement in place with her doctor to make the end come relatively quickly. This would have involved morphine injections, which along with quelling pain, also serve to depress the respiratory system, thus speeding the onset of pneumonia. But administering morphine to a patient not in extreme pain is a quasi-legal practice, and few medical practitioners will do it without clear discretionary powers assured by the family.

It was here that the error was made. In their initial meeting with my mother's doctor, one of my sisters, likely distraught at seeing my mother's condition, let the following sentence drop: *"Isn't there something we can do?"*

The medical system has a ready answer to this question. Medical measures are available that could stabilize my mother's condition. These measures—mechanical rehydration, intravenous administering of nutrients, along with a host of drugs that might or might not stabilize the bleeding inside her brain and prevent further damage—might have prolonged her life indefinitely in a semivegetative state. Stroke victims can linger in this kind of limbo for months, years. In extreme cases, a decade or more can pass.

The doctor discreetly didn't answer my sister's question. But discretion and caution are one and the same in geriatric medicine, and he wisely withdrew from the situation—I didn't see him again until close to the end. The completely innocent of-the-moment question my sister asked raised the issue of how onside the family actually was with the No Heroic Measures agreement, and it wasn't something that could be clarified, even in private, because it would require the doctor to ask us some questions of his own that would expose him to legal liability if one of us subsequently changed our mind. Worse, the fundamentalist nurses in the hospital who were present when the question was asked had been liberated by it to countermand the NHM order, and would be hawking my mother's doctor's interactions with her. That question my sister asked—which was less a question than an expression of regret—made my mother a battle piece in a medical culture war, and it condemned her to an excruciating death.

We couldn't ask her if she was still onside because she couldn't communicate beyond that shrug. We tried to put together a rudimentary communication system—one eye blink for yes, two for no, but the stroke seemed to have disabled her ability to process language. She knew who we were, she knew who she was, but I don't think she could understand what we were saying, and was incapable of articulating her thoughts.

Yet within the first 36 hours, she found ways to communicate to us that she hadn't changed her mind about dying. Serena left the room for a few minutes while a nurse was changing the sheets and returned to find the nurse trying to spoon Pablum between my mother's lips—and to find my mother refusing to swallow, even summonsing the will to blow the gruel across the sheets. On a shift a few hours later, Nina ducked out for a breath of fresh air while my mother slept, and returned to discover that a nurse had placed an intravenous needle in my mother's arm—and to witness my mother pawing frantically to remove it.

One of us—Ron, probably, who'd taken on a kind of calm authority in the first few days that commanded everyone's respect—

explained patiently to the nurses that we were serious about the No Heroic Measures order, and we agreed among ourselves not to leave the room unguarded while certain nurses were present.

And so the days began to pass. Nieces and nephews showed up to sit vigil—my son Max, then at university in Vancouver and in the middle of his exams, caught a bus and spent a day at his grandmother's bedside, and so did Nina's daughter Laura, on whom my mother had conferred the de facto role of the next keeper of family solidarities. There was also a steady stream of my mother's friends. Most were elderly, but a few younger women showed up, including, one afternoon, her investment counsellor. It was gratifying but not quite surprising, and it helped to pass the hours. My mother seemed to recognize everyone, gave each of them her shrug of greeting— look what's become of me—but her language was gone.

My sisters bullied my father into making one trip down to the hospital—but just the one. He walked through the hospital rotunda as if it were a prison panopticon, followed us meekly to my mother's ward. Then he stood in the doorway of her room and gazed at her in silence until she noticed he was there. He mouthed a few uncomfortable pleasantries, briefly held her hand, and left within 20 minutes. He seemed shaken, and soon after we returned to the house, he broke down, wandering around the living room muttering and weeping.

We got him to sit down, and Nina leaned over him, put her arms around his shoulders and asked him what was bothering him.

"Rita's been with me for 60 years," he answered, bursting into tears again. "And now what's going to become of me?"

Nina stepped back as if she'd been slapped. "For God's sake, Dad," she snapped. "This is happening to Mum, not to you!"

"I've got to think ahead," my father mumbled, his expression chastened but not guilty in the least. "It's going to be awful lonely around here."

*   *   *

My night shifts proved less trying than I thought. They were, actually, easier than some of the shifts during the day: few nurses were on duty at night, and my mother, at first, seemed less restive than during the day, sleeping soundly for three and even four hours at a stretch. When she was awake, I talked to her, and when that ran out, I read to her. It didn't seem to matter which I did, although she wanted eye contact more while I was reading. I was never sure she understood what I was saying, but she did recognize interrogatives, to which she responded by raising her eyebrows in an interrogative of her own. It wasn't "Why me?" but rather an almost-joking "Isn't this awful, here we are together in the middle of the night, and we can't talk."

Can a person dying this way be comforted in any meaningful way? My voice seemed to calm her agitation only a little, and there were moments when I almost convinced myself that she understood what I was saying to her. Eye contact clearly calmed her, and so did touch, but talking was easier, and so I talked, and talked.

I'd also brought a tape player with me, and I played her a tape I'd compiled for her months earlier for a Christmas present. Her favourites were there, Nelson Eddy and Jeanette MacDonald singing "Sweet Mystery of Life," and *Cavalleria Rusticana*, about which I learned, from watching her eyes as it played, that it was only the intermezzo that she knew and loved. I'd added a new recording by Rufus Wainwright of Irving Berlin's "What'll I Do," which she responded to by lifting and dropping her good arm several times in a way that left me undecided whether she was pleased or upset by it. But the song that moved her most was a 1950s recording of Kitty Kallen singing "Little Things Mean a Lot." I'd found a 45 of it in a second-hand record store back in the summer, and bought it without quite knowing why until a few days later when a memory snapshot restored itself.

I'd been about ten years old the first time I heard the song. My mother and I were at home listening to the morning radio when the song came on. She was tidying the living room, and she stopped and listened raptly, with a dreamy, troubled look on her face. She returned to the kitchen, and I followed her, sitting at the kitchen table as she busied herself at the sink, fussing with the dishes and keeping her face averted.

When she turned around there were tears running down her cheeks, and now, 40 years later, I saw the tears again. She lifted her arm and dropped it, and I understood that she wanted me to play it again. I cued the machine, and this time, I listened to the lyrics:

> *Blow me a kiss from across the room*
> *Say I look nice when I'm not*
> *Touch my hair as you pass my chair*
> *Little things mean a lot*
>
> *Give me your arm as we cross the street*
> *Call me at six on the dot*
> *A line a day when you're far away*
> *Little things mean a lot*
>
> *Give me a hand when I've lost the way*
> *Give me your shoulder to cry on*
> *Whether the day is bright or gray*
> *Give me your heart to rely on*
>
> *Send me the warmth of a secret smile*
> *To show me you haven't forgot*
> *For now and forever, always and ever*
> *Little things mean a lot.*

As I listened to Kallen's achy voice, I realized that this wasn't just my mother's song. It was my summary—on her behalf—of the things my father had never done to please her.

Did this mean she'd had an unhappy marriage? No. She'd gotten most of the things she wanted from it: healthy children she saw grow up, a community that appreciated her, a quiet life free of deprivation, a couple of Cadillacs to ride in—even if the last one advertised "Barley Max" on the side doors. She'd gotten domestic partnership, and a strong one. What she hadn't gotten was companionship and the daily affection that could have made the partnership sweet. I don't think she had deep regrets beyond those little things. But like the song says, little things mean a lot.

So I shed some tears with her as we listened to Kitty Kallen, but when I felt them coming I moved myself beyond her visual range. She didn't need to see that I was upset. She'd have wanted to comfort me, and she had troubles of her own. This time, the troubles were mortal in the most profound way.

*   *   *

I had to remind myself a few more times as the days passed that this wasn't about me any more than it was about my father. Sure, it's a hard thing to watch your mother die, and there's nothing on earth that can prepare you for it. No platitudes or 12-step programs help you. You can't hide from the reality that a person you've loved all your life is dying when you're witnessing the physical facts of impending death progress day by day and hour by hour. I was determined to comfort her in whatever small ways I could, and not make it about me. What made it slightly easier to focus on my job was that I was also, quietly and with the barest sort of self-awareness, growing angry. It was dawning on me that I was able neither to help nor comfort the woman who'd spent her life helping and comforting me, and that what my siblings and I had agreed to had become a waking nightmare.

Like most nightmares, this one carried its own self-propelling logic, and there was no way for us to alter that logic. We could continue what had been started, which was to subject her to the gruesome suffering of starvation and dehydration until she died from it, or we could bring the process to a stop, contravene her wishes, and prolong her agony indefinitely, although at a lesser intensity. Neither choice was a decent one.

The sole guide available to us was that her will was unwavering even though her route to the end was becoming more excruciating as the hours passed. To the extent that she was able to communicate at all, this was the one thing about which her wishes were unambiguous.

But why weren't there other choices? If it is the victim's decision not to continue living, why wasn't euthanasia possible?

I'll tell you. It is because Canada and most other Western countries are in the grip of a medical fundamentalism that unilaterally imposes duration of life on the elderly over quality of life. This fundamentalism is largely lodged in religious values, although some civil libertarians contribute by pointing to the slippery moral slope that becomes visible when the idea of state-sanctioned euthanasia is broached. Those concerns could be dealt with in ways similar to the way most civilized societies now handle abortion: by making it a decision to be taken between patient and doctor, with the state barred from declaring it either legal or illegal. What everyone misses in this is that at the root of the way we approach the end of life for the elderly are powerful economic and technological currents, and that these are powerful enough to supersede, by and large, the moral stances we can take.

None of our religious institutions, calcified as they are by nearly a century of struggle against the militant materialism of Karl Marx

and the Bolshevik materialism that Vladimir Lenin constructed
from Marx's theoretical writings, can offer anyone nuanced choices
about the fundamental issues of life and death in the twenty-first
century. Institutions like the Roman Catholic Church (which
attempts to ascribe all authority to the Church and its domestically
illiterate clerics) and a thousand other demagogic restorationist
protestantisms (which most often are on a bloody-minded quest to
return all moral and legal authority to literal and mostly specious
interpretations of the Bible) help no one with this. Each, in different ways, are mired in notions of the sanctity of human life that
are rooted in the humanism of the Renaissance. These same senile
institutions were able to ignore the nearly 100 million who were
murdered during the twentieth century in the name of ethnic, racial,
and political reasoning. They now ignore—or exacerbate—the
insane overpopulating of the planet that we are now perpetrating.
We who live under their miasma ignore the truth that all of these
institutions are run for profit, not for the dignity of individual life
or for collective well-being. Religious doctrine in the twenty-first
century is designed, more than ever before, to legitimize the authority of the religious institutions, and virtually every sensible person
knows this—in an utterly powerless way.

Meanwhile, advances in medical science have given medical
practitioners and the bureaucratic and industrial apologists of
medical technology powerful abilities to prolong human life. This
has occurred without even the most rudimentary cultural conversation about how or where to deploy the advances, and with little
discussion of what constitutes a life worth prolonging or who has
the legitimate authority to choose termination or prolongation, and
under what circumstances. Thus, the medical technology itself,
tacitly backed by the churches, makes these choices for us, often
by extending the lives of people who don't want to continue them,
and by tormenting their families and loved loves with interstitial

decisions that aren't decisions at all. Like most technology, life-prolonging medical technology is deployed simply because it exists and (this is equally important) because its deployment will generate profits for those who create and manufacture it. Yes, the idea of an alliance between religious fundamentalism and sophisticated corporate technology is counterintuitive. But after a half century inside the nightmare that was the nuclear arms race, where the cultural alliance was virtually identical, no one should be surprised by it.

Few of us understand what this alliance does on a daily basis. But when you spend two weeks in a hospital watching it torture an innocent woman who happens to be your mother, you see it in a new way. It is not benign, not civilized. It is a new kind of barbarism.

My siblings and I did what we'd agreed to do—each of us in our own way, and with our own misgivings. We shared some of our grief, each of us marvellously careful not to make a special case for what we were feeling. We also shared, to a lesser extent, the anger that was breeding in each of us, along with the sense of helplessness that was feeding it.

At the end of the first week, my mother began to fade. She slept more, she was less responsive: we saw the shrug less frequently. This decline was what passed for mercy. For my sisters, who had both become—if such a thing is possible—devout Anglicans during the previous decade, this *was* God's late-in-coming mercy. For my brother and me, it was simply relief from her suffering, and from us having to witness her pain, from having to experience it by proxy. But along with the relief was a growing sense of guilt, and an objectless rage.

I talked on the phone nightly with my wife Leanna and my then three-year-old daughter, Hartlea, who asked me to kiss her grandmother for her so she'd get better. I could barely communicate with them because outside the hospital, at my parents' house and on the route to and fro, I had difficulty staying in control of my emotions.

I burst into tears in the local mall without warning, I screamed at an inattentive gas station clerk, I was overly effusive with the Canadian Tire clerk who sold me a Christmas tree, which I put up in the house against my father's wishes, festooned with new strings of lights I bought and decorated with some old ornaments I scrounged from the crawlspace in the basement.

At the hospital I gave up playing the music tape and mostly read poetry aloud, or talked about whatever inane things passed through my head. There were more and more moments when I wasn't sure she knew who I was—some person there to keep her company—nice enough, but she was passing beyond identity, maybe because her pain was inducing an anaesthetized lassitude that overwhelmed it.

As the eighth day ended, we asked for, and got, periodic morphine injections to ease her deepening physical distress. She wasn't there profoundly enough to be able to use a self-administered morphine drip, nor were any of us willing to risk the inevitable temptations such a device would have presented. The nurses were reluctant to administer morphine because they knew better than we that it would trigger pneumonia. But we persisted, playing their own ethos at them, which proscribed, at least, the kind of convulsive pain she was experiencing.

And so she sank into the abyss that was her approaching death, and we into its accompanying morass of regret and guilt and unbidden recollection. When death was in plain sight, a space came up in the hospice attached to the hospital. It was too late for my mother to appreciate the muted decor, soft lighting, and the absence of hallway echoes and banging medical and food carts, but I had to admit that she'd have liked the hospice. Except for the several vases of artificial flowers and the lack of broadloom on the floors—even palliative care can be messy—the decor wasn't terribly different than the decor in the house up on the hill.

So the hospice was for our comfort, and we were relieved to have gotten there, if not quite comforted. It meant, for one thing, an end to the fundamentalist nurses trying to spoon-feed my mother and jam IVs into her arms, and it meant that her death would be private, free from the impersonal clatter of hospital routine. In some curious ways, it also returned all of us to the world. The morning she was moved, it snowed again. As the ambulance crew lifted her from the van, snowflakes alighted on her face, and I saw her eyes blink, then close, as if the tactile sensation was too much a reminder that the world still existed.

An hour later the sky cleared. When I went outside in the crystalled brilliance of the afternoon sunlight, I recalled how beautiful the world was, how blue the sky, how green the dark pines that dotted the hillside above the hospital, how persistent and ordinary the lives of the people outside our cocoon of dying: they went to their jobs, their geriatric exercise classes, they drove to the mall to shop—all as if nothing we were experiencing was real, or if it was real, that it didn't matter.

It also came to me that first afternoon at the hospice, that we might have innocently done something—or neglected to do something—that might have made my mother's decline more cruel than it needed to be. For at least the last decade she'd suffered from fairly serious acid reflux, a condition in which, while lying prone, stomach acid migrates into the esophagus and throat. For years now she had slept with a triangular bolster that kept her head elevated above her torso, using simple gravity to prevent the stomach acids from migrating. None of us had thought to mention this condition to the doctors or nurses, and they'd hardly have known about it without a deep search into her medical records, since the condition was longstanding, and may not have even been recorded.

How to handle this now? Should I bring it up this late in her ordeal and load a further burden of guilt on my sisters and brothers?

If my mother had suffered from it earlier in this gruesome palliative descent—and it was likely that she had, given the human stomach's slightly perverse capacity to produce acids in search of food—that misery had since been overwhelmed by greater ones, and it was likely that her stomach had now more or less given up and shut itself down. So I said nothing, let it infuse within my private guilt and anger. For all I knew, I might have been the last of us to figure it out, and my siblings had been according me the same perverse mercy I was now conceding to them.

It wasn't until the afternoon of December 11, when she slipped into what would be a permanent coma, that I was truly certain that death would come. The preceding days had become a blur: the siege of nurses and doctors, the daily dustings of snow in the parking lot, the tense family conferences that could decide on nothing worthwhile except funeral arrangements. That night I wrote the obituary, along with several eulogies that I tore up as soon as they were on paper: ghoulish. My brother and sisters and I ate, slept, and drove back and forth to the hospital like automatons. I caught myself thinking that it would go on forever because it already felt as if it had gone on forever.

Yet I also understood that it *was* ending. My mother's breathing was slowing, becoming more ragged and laboured, her pallor deepening, her bodily tissues visibly collapsing. And except for convulsive near-awakenings, coma reigned and glimmers of pneumonia were visible. The old person's friend, it is called, but it seemed anything but friendly. It was malevolent and heavy, its bacterial growth the final violent attack on her fading vitality. She had been starved and dehydrated, and now pneumonia was coming to drown her.

The clinical description of how pneumonia does its work is worth noting:

The microbes of pneumonia lie in wait for the appearance of any added insult that might inhibit further the already-damaged defenses of the aged. Coma is their perfect ally. It takes away every conscious way of resisting their predations, and even destroys so basic a safety device as the cough reflex. Any bit of regurgitation or foreign matter that under ordinary circumstances would be forcefully ejected at the first sign of its invasion of the airway now becomes the vehicle on which the germs ride triumphantly into the respiratory tissues. The microscopic air sacs called alveoli then swell and are destroyed by inflammation. As a result, the proper exchange of gases is prevented, and blood oxygen diminishes while carbon dioxide may build up until vital functions can no longer be sustained. When oxygen levels drop below a critical point, the brain manifests it by further cell death, and the heart by fibrillation or arrest. Pneumonia triumphs.

Late that afternoon, one of the palliative care nurses suggested to us that it wouldn't be long—an hour, she said, or a day. But not days. "Most likely tonight," she said, adding, "depending on how strong she is."

Then it won't be today, I thought. Late tonight, perhaps, but more likely, tomorrow. I had no opinion, expert or otherwise, about when it should happen, not sooner, because then I would lose her, but not later, because her suffering was no more acceptable than it had been a week ago, and the epic labour to simply breathe on had become a horror.

I stayed at the hospice most of the day—we all did—and then ducked out around eight in the evening for some sleep before the night shift. My sister Nina didn't leave at all, napping fitfully instead on a small wicker couch under the picture window across from the bed.

When I arrived around midnight, my mother's labour had deepened, but it seemed to have stabilized. I tried to read but couldn't, and about 4 a.m., when Nina woke up, I drove back to the house for another hour or two of sleep.

I was pulled from that by the phone. I staggered from the couch I was sleeping on and picked up. It was my brother.

"It's happening," he said. "You should come."

The four of us paced around the deathbed for several hours, barely able to speak as each breath she took became an act of hero-ism, each one rattling out brokenly as if it was going to be, had to be, the last. There was little left of the woman who had borne us into the world, nothing of her vitality or her laughter, replaced instead by this labouring vessel that couldn't possible persist another minute and yet did, awfully, in a rhythmic insanity that was at once life's humiliation and its grandeur.

And then the rhythm slowed, grew, impossibly, more ragged and chaotic, broke down for a moment, then reified, then sank, then stopped, then skidded forward, then drew itself up, a gulping in of oxygen, released without being taken, with an audible, catastrophic, epic shudder,

and stopped forever.

*   *   *

It was worse than I've been able to describe. And worse still was the 30 or 40 seconds that followed, where each of us hoped that there would be another breath—and just as fervently hoped that there wouldn't be.

There wasn't.

Christmas Time: But First, a Funeral

***

THREE HUNDRED PEOPLE came to the funeral. About 50 were family, and another 30 or 40 were people I recognized but whose names hadn't ever registered. But the rest, who knows? Most of the funeral logistics had been handled by my sisters, but I didn't recall them phoning more than a dozen people. Then I remembered the obituary, which I'd delivered to the newspaper in the aftermath fog, with instructions to run it for two days. In a town like Penticton with its elderly majority, the obituaries are the paper's most-read section.

My mother was well liked in her community. In her last years, she had, like many older people do, worked harder at being likeable, and not just by recounting every good deed she'd done to everyone who'd listen. She'd always been good at working a crowd, and as a hospital volunteer, she'd gotten better at one-to-one with strangers. People liked her, and why wouldn't they? She never whined about old age and the infirmities it brought, and her natural sweetness and her good manners masked her steely shrewdness better than ever. Her investment counsellor showed up too, a young woman in her late twenties, and I don't think she was in tears only because she was losing my mother's portfolio.

But three hundred? I don't know that many people, let alone expect them to come to my funeral.

I'd been occupied with catching up on sleep and getting my part of the family there. Jesse, my oldest son, flew in, and Leanna and Hartlea managed to get a flight out of Toronto hours after my mother died. I'd gratefully driven the 60 kilometres north to Kelowna to pick them all up. Max, who'd already bused up while his grandmother was still alive, opted to write his exams, and I didn't object. He'd said his goodbyes while she could still wave back at him. Nearly everyone in the extended family showed up, a full motel of them, even though there'd been no pressure applied.

They knew how to do funerals in Penticton, and why wouldn't they? There were enough funerals that the mourners understand the balance between grief and celebrating the life just ended. Nearly everyone in the church was dressed in black or other muted colours, but most were chattering away at one another, albeit with enough tears flowing to make it respectful. And anyway, when an old friend dies at 90 years of age, part of what you're doing at the funeral is covering your bets for your own. Losing the presence of someone like my mother in the community is cause for regret, sure, but her death wasn't really a major interruption of human possibilities. Her possibilities had largely been explored, and everyone seemed to understand that she'd gone without regrets.

My siblings and I had been discovering, in the three days between her death and the funeral, just how prepared she'd been. The living will had been just one part of it. Her legal will, when we rescued it from her safety deposit box, was a masterpiece of careful detail, designed with a single goal: to keep us from fighting over the estate, which was quite a lot larger than anyone expected, including my father. She'd managed, over the decades, to accumulate a sizable portfolio of annuities and bonds, which the will told us exactly how and where to locate. All of it was to be divided equally, as were the contents of the house. At the bottom of the will, in capital letters, was this message to us all, written in her hand: NO FIGHTING!

When we read that, we burst out laughing—our first collective laugh in two weeks, and not a trace of it was cynical. But how determined she was to see it go as she'd dictated became evident as we gradually discovered that virtually everything in the house that was even remotely valuable or attractive had one of our names written on the back of it, or underneath it. She didn't want *any* fighting.

We were each, in different ways, too exhausted to fight over anything even if we wanted to. And when we weren't, we were too angry and upset at the travesty we'd just seen to its terrible end to think about crossing her or one another. The graceful and painless exit she'd planned for herself had gone brutally wrong, so the least we could do was make the aftermath go according to her wishes, and that included conducting the funeral exactly the way she wanted it.

We executed the funeral according to her instruction sheet, all the way down to hiring an almost-in-tune soloist to murder "Breathe on Me Breath of God." Then we lined up three or four eulogies, including one each from my brother and me. Both of us tried to tell the truth about her as we knew it, and both of us, about halfway through, lost our composure and blubbered our way to the end of what we were trying to say, still far too close to what we'd just witnessed to hold ourselves together.

Nobody seemed to mind our blubbering, and the two women who spoke after us, one from the hospital auxiliary and a younger woman from the local Beta Sigma Phi chapter my mother had grandmothered, fell apart when they spoke, too. My sisters, never much for making speeches, stayed in their seats, and so did my dry-eyed father, who spent most of the service rubbernecking. Then the local Anglican priest blathered on for a few minutes about the arms of the Lord and the Glories of Heaven, then read the formal liturgy

as if what had happened was supposed to be a good and sweet elevation of being. I recalled that my mother had been quite a lot less than
completely fond of this man, and that he hadn't shown up at the
hospital to check out what sort of elevation her being was getting. If
he had, I doubt that he'd have been rattling on the way he was.

But no one seemed to mind his platitudes, and when he was
done, everyone repaired to the church basement to munch on sandwiches, coffee, and tea and talk about how much they were going to
miss Rita Fawcett. I got a lot of "there-theres" deposited on my
shoulders, and I tried to pretend that I recognized the depositors.
I did take some comfort from the warmth of it, and even found
myself admiring the ones who were probably wondering, in the
backs of their minds, if they were going to be the next to be feted
this way.

We'd also planned a smaller wake the following day, mainly for
family, but we also invited a couple dozen of my parents' closest
friends. At the end of it, after the outsiders left, we planned to read
the will aloud to the assembled family, and then let the women
divide up my mother's clothing and jewellery. Between the four of
us we'd already agreed that we weren't going to take any of the
household stuff, none of the furniture, and only a few of the mementoes apportioned to us in the will. My father still had a life to live,
and we didn't want to disrupt it any more than it had already been.

My father had spent much of his time before the funeral napping, staying out of everyone's way, and muttering darkly about
where my mother had accumulated "all that goddamned money."
When he wasn't doing that he was spending a lot of time on the
phone trying to cadge dinner invitations for the weeks after we left.
He seemed more agitated than stricken by grief, but I couldn't tell
if that was a result of the tongue-lashing he'd received after his sole
visit to the hospital, or whether he really didn't give a damn.

It wasn't either of those, as it turned out. He was formulating, rapidly and ruthlessly, his plan for the future. If I'd been paying attention, I'd have gotten a taste for exactly how ruthless his plan was, too. About two months before my mother had the stroke, he'd finally given up his driver's licence and sold off his big green Cadillac. Now, with no one to drive him here and there, he wanted the licence back, and something to drive.

This was not a good idea in anyone's mind but his, because he'd long been a menace on the roads, virtually blind, mostly deaf, and with an attitude that anyone who didn't like his driving style was a careless sonofabitch in too much of a hurry. A couple of Thanksgivings before, I'd brought then infant Hartlea to Penticton to show her to the family for the first time, and made the mistake of letting him pick us up at the airport. He drove the kilometre-long stretch from the terminal to the highway at 20 kilometres an hour on the wrong side of the road. It was midday, but he didn't care, swearing at the several cars that pulled over to the margins, horns blaring: What the hell do they want? When he ran the stoplight and made a left turn into the main highway's oncoming lane, I decided that I cared enough that I never again got into a car he was driving.

Here he insisted that I drive him down to the motor-vehicle office, where, in less than ten minutes, he alternately bullyragged and then tearjerked the bewildered clerk into reinstating his driving privileges on compassionate grounds: his wife had just died, and he was isolated and poor. It seems there was a provision for this that the clerk didn't know about but which my father, himself pretending to be on the edge of tears, successfully insisted was at the clerk's discretion. Then he bullied me into transferring the ownership of my mother's car to him for $100, getting by my objections by promising to have the cataract operations he'd been avoiding, while arguing that paying anything more for an old heap like her car was highway robbery. The car was a ten-year-old compact we both knew was worth considerably more than $100, but never mind that.

He managed to hold his driver's licence for six more years without killing anyone—although he once forgot to engage the parking gear and had to watch as the little car rolled across the street, up the driveway of a neighbour and through his garage door. It was early in the morning and the neighbour was out of town, so my father walked across the street, retrieved the slightly damaged car, and pretended innocence later that day when the suspicious neighbour asked him if he'd seen what happened. He hadn't heard a thing, he said, pointing out that he was barely able to see enough to drive his own car, let alone act as the local watchdog.

The wake was as cheerfully uneventful as the funeral had been. Everyone there, Protestants to the bone, was as lightheartedly determined to celebrate her life as her four children were unwilling to inflict the horror of her death on them. That the reading of her will gave $10,000 to each of her ten grandchildren leavened their spirits considerably, not that this was needed. The crowning event of the evening was when the 20 or so females in the extended family retreated to her bedroom and amidst much laughter, told stories about her while they took turns picking their favourite things of hers. My mother would have enjoyed every moment of that, particularly when there was very little left after they were done.

There was just the one sour note, and my father provided it. While the rest of us comforted one another with silly stories and ate sandwiches left over from the church-basement reception, my father stood in the kitchen and made phone calls to a list of women he'd drawn up, wondering if they might want to move in with him. When he phoned a woman in Prince George he'd sold the family house to 20 years ago, and about whom there had been some suspicions after he'd sold it to her well below its market value, my sister

Serena, normally the most even-tempered of us, ushered him outside and exploded.

"For God's sake, Dad," she roared, loud enough that everyone inside could hear her. "Mum hasn't been gone for four days and you're trying to pick up women at her wake? What on earth is wrong with you?"

My father was cowed, but he wasn't contrite. "I have to arrange a housekeeper," he answered. "I don't imagine any of you are going to take care of me."

Serena wasn't having any of it. "You weren't asking them to be your housekeeper. And you can bloody well wait a week or two before you move in one of your girlfriends. Show some respect."

He didn't make any more phone calls that day, but it was plain to all of us that he wasn't listening, either. He was reacting to the end of his life with my mother like a man just released from prison: by rapidly, openly, and almost giddily attempting to get on with the rest of his life. At the top of his agenda—this was a man who hated to be alone, remember—was companionship. Trying to pick up women at the funeral reception was only part of it, and my sisters continued to take an extremely dim view of his behaviour and his general attitude. I didn't understand what he was up to either, and found myself wondering if he'd lost his marbles.

A complete break between my father and me was, at that moment, a possibility for the first time in my life. My mother, you see, had imposed a non-negotiable rule at the centre of our family life when the first of us reached adolescence. She told us that we could fight as much as we wanted, any and all of us, but we still had to come home. It had been one of her ways of preserving the family in the face of my father's often clumsy and aggressive attempts to control us, and I suppose it was also her way of getting around the stubbornness and stupidity of people in adult bodies without adult minds. She made it clear that there was nothing any of us could have done with our lives horrible enough to get us exiled. There was probably a line somewhere across which we couldn't go, but she made a fair show of trusting our good natures not to. None of us had ever challenged the rule or come within a country mile of the ultimate penalty.

But now that she was dead, I *could* break contact with my father, thus ending our long war and, not incidentally, making him the scapegoat for my helpless rage, punishing him for what I hadn't been able to do to protect my mother. I'll admit that I was looking for someone or something to blame. I couldn't talk to my sisters about it. They were leaning on their rebirthed belief in God to get them through the mess we'd made, and I was thinking any God that allowed such cruelty as we'd just witnessed wasn't anything more than a target to throw custard pies at. My brother and I saw things more similarly, but we hadn't been getting along for a long time and this wasn't the time to resolve our differences—if they could be resolved at all.

The most sensitive and emotionally reserved of us, my brother was putting on a brave front despite his unresolved issues with his mother, who he half believed hadn't ever adequately connected with him because, well, she'd preferred me or my sisters. This had come up in the last few days at the hospice, and I'd tried to explain to him that she'd always practised a scrupulous emotional democracy amongst us, and that what he saw as her lack of interest was the dynamic of having had three children within 18 months of one another, of whom the elder two were identical twins and he was, by nature as well as seniority, the less-demanding third. But it *was* true that the two of them had never quite worked it out, and at the moment of her death I was almost as moved by his evident pain at losing her with that unresolved as by my own private loss. There was no way I could communicate any of this to him.

The afternoon before I left Penticton, my brother and sisters drove down to the mall to shop for groceries, I sent Leanna and Hartlea after them, and my father and I had it out. I told him that I didn't like the way he'd treated my mother, that I'd never liked it, but that his behaviour since her stroke was unforgivable.

"How dare you try to pick up women in the middle of your own wife's wake!" I snarled. "You were married for a long time, and you should have at least had the decency to wait until the family wasn't around before you start screwing around."

My father listened to my tirade with an uncharacteristic calmness. "Are you finished?" he asked, when I—and my rage—began to run down. "Because I need you to hear my side, for once."

"Okay," I said, still bristling. "I'm listening."

"I'm 93 years old," he said. There was a directness in his voice that I'd never in my life heard from him before. "I don't have much time left. I could be dead in six months, or in two years. I'll be lucky if I get much more than that. Very lucky."

I began to object, but he waved it away, held my gaze, and maintained the same almost-pleading tone. "Your mother and I have been fighting for 50 years, and as you already know, my feelings are pretty mixed about her. I imagine they're as mixed as yours are about me right now."

I nodded, but kept my mouth shut.

"Your sisters," he said, "talk about a decent interval. I don't have time for a decent interval. I have to get on with my life now because it's going to be over pretty soon and I want some joy and happiness before I go, if I can find it. You kids can do whatever you think is best, but whether you like it or not, I'm going to go out there and find someone, and try to make it someone I can be happy with. I don't have time to wait, and I'm not going to waste a minute of what I do have. I can't tell you what to do with this, so I'm not going to try. I just wanted you to hear my point of view."

He was finished, and he stood in front of me like a child, waiting. For the life of me, I couldn't think of an answer. It wasn't a question of believing him. I did. What I couldn't get around was myself. The anger and shame I was feeling was too front and centre, too raw and, maybe, too compelling to allow me to think straight let alone figure out what I was feeling about him. I could tell him it was all okay, or I could insist on continuing the war as my mother's proxy. Rage prevented the former, but the logic of what he'd just said and his vulnerability made the latter feel like cruelty.

What I did was nothing at all. I drove to Kelowna the next morning, got on the plane with the wife and daughter I loved, and flew home to Toronto. I told myself I'd never come back but I knew I would. That duty was intact, cemented in place by my father's plea for understanding.

Christmas? Well, Christmas came and went. When we got back to Toronto I put up half the outdoor lights I normally festoon the house with, but we put up the same lavishly decorated oversized tree as always. I cooked a turkey—unbrined—and stuffed the way my mother had taught me, and I moped my way through to New Year's and the beginning of the twenty-first century. The holiday season wasn't made brighter by the parcel of small gifts—including the net bag of kids' trinkets—my mother had mailed a few hours before the stroke.

A Wedding

HARTLEY FAWCETT was as good as his word: he didn't waste a minute. He was better than his word, actually. He uncovered much more than mere companionship. He found several women to love him, one who was willing to marry him, and he turned his life from a strife-filled business melodrama into a glorious comedy that lasted seven full years.

It never felt like a farce, his comedy, although there was plenty of slapstick. It was classical comedy, pulling in all of the etymological roots of the Greek word: revelry, and singing in the village. Yet it was often straight out of Shakespeare, with tensions between truth and desire, separations and reunifications, mistaken identities that were rectified, and the gradual, glorious elevation of who is really who and what happiness means.

My father had always been happy, but his happiness had been impossible to extract from his oblivious self-involvement and his business bullshit. This was different: he needed other people now, in ways he never had before, and he began to see people not as something to manipulate or subjugate to his will, but as themselves.

His plan for companionship was simple: he courted any woman who'd give him the time of day. He got himself out of the house

early and late to cruise the card games at the local seniors' recre-
ation centre, and though the wildlife he found there may not have
seemed like swans to most people, to him, all females became beau-
ties. At the best of times, dating after you've been in a long marriage
can be unsettling: What do you say to a stranger while you're
preparing to be intimate; or worse, what do you do when you are?
How can you be intimate at all with a new person after decades of
familiarity with another? When you're in the over-80 demographic
there are additional hazards, and not all are about physical limita-
tions and ossified emotional circuitry. Yet somehow, none of this
hindered my father.

His first serious girlfriend was a
woman over 80, a woman he quickly
discovered was mildly afflicted by the
onset of Alzheimer's. No problem
with that. Conversation was easily
made because it was quickly forgotten. Better yet from his point of
view, among the things that dementia dissolves in human personality
are sexual inhibitions.

When Leanna and I flew out for
Thanksgiving that fall, my father,
still wary of me, quickly cornered
her, eager to confide. They ended up in his study while I cooked
dinner, but I could hear them talking animatedly down the hallway. Mostly it was my father's voice I heard, punctuated by hoots
of laughter from Leanna. After about 20 minutes, they reappeared.
Leanna looked a little flustered.

"Dad, really," I heard her say, laughing. "Don't you think this
might be a little too much information?"

After she stopped laughing, which was hours later, she told me what they'd been talking about—or rather what he'd been monologuing over.

"Your father has discovered oral sex," she said.

"Really."

"Yes. Really."

"What does he call it?"

"He doesn't have a name for it. But he certainly seems to like it."

"Which way is it going?"

"Oh, his way, I'm pretty sure."

"What about the other way?"

Leanna laughed out loud. "It was hard enough trying to keep a straight face as it was," she said. "I didn't ask."

"Didn't you mention that people with Alzheimer's have difficulty with impulse control?"

"I didn't know they did," she said. "And anyway . . ."

"What does her family think about all this?"

"I don't know that either. It was hard to get a word in edgewise."

The woman's family, it turned out, *was* thinking about it, probably because they understood that she was farther along the dementia path than my father realized. When I talked to him close to Christmas, I asked how things were going.

"Not so good," he said, cheerfully. "I had to get rid of my girl-friend."

"Oh?" I said. "Why's that?"

"Her mind was starting to go," he said. "She started hitting me with things for no reason. And half the time, she didn't know who the hell I was. Life's too bloody short for that sort of nonsense."

"I know what you mean," I said.

There was a pause at the other end of the line.

"Well, *I* didn't know there was that kind of nonsense."

Another pause. "We had some good times," he said, with real regret in his voice. "But it was time to move on."

Move on he did. The following March I received a long-distance call from Penticton. A woman, clearly an older woman from the sound of her voice, was on the other end of the line. "My name is Georgie," she said. "I'm going to be in Toronto visiting my cousin next week. I'd like to talk to you about your father."

"Call me when you get in," I said. "And we'll set something up."

I hung up, and called my sister Nina, who'd recently been in Penticton, and asked her if she knew anything about a woman named Georgie.

"She's your father's latest girlfriend," she said. "I think he's quite serious about her."

"Serious?" I asked. "What does that mean?"

"I think he's asked her to marry him."

"How old is she?"

"She's about 70," Nina said. "Or so."

"Doesn't she know Dad's almost 95?"

"Dad says she doesn't care." There was a pause on the other end of the line. "So what was I *supposed* to tell him? He's not going to listen anyway. I told him, good luck."

When Georgie called me back a week later from a Toronto number, I invited her over for dinner. She appeared at the front door at the agreed time, a small, sweet-faced woman with iron-grey permed hair, not the sort of woman who'd ever been a beauty. But her eyes were bright and intelligent, and she carried herself with a directness that was disarming.

She'd come to ask my permission to marry my father. She came to me, I suspected, because she'd calculated that I was going to be the hardest nut to crack: I'd been closest to my mother, and I'd had the most difficult relationship with her husband-to-be. But this wasn't quite calculation on her part. It was courtesy, and given that she had no way of knowing how I'd react, it was impossible not to admire her for it.

In the spirit of the event, I asked her several direct questions: "You do know that Dad is 95, don't you? Aren't you worried about the age difference?"

"No," she said, gazing back at me without a hint of guile. "I have a heart condition and diabetes. I'm only 70, but no one in my family has gotten past their mid-seventies. He'll probably outlive me."

She looked down for a moment, as if trying to decide how to articulate what she was going to say next. "I was married once," she continued. "But I've lived alone for 35 years. I don't *need* to get married to your father. I'm financially independent. I don't need anyone's money, and I've always been able to take care of myself. But, you know, I love your father. He's good to me. He's made me happier than I thought I could be, and I want to live out the rest of my life with him, however long that's going to be."

They were married in late May, although Georgie moved in a week after she returned from Toronto. None of us was *delighted* at the thought of our father remarrying, but since it was making him happy, what was there to object to?

I flew into Kelowna three days before the wedding with Leanna and my now five-year-old daughter. We rented a car and drove to Penticton, more prepared to endure the festivities than to enjoy them. Georgie insisted that the three of us stay at the house, arguing that since we'd come the farthest, we shouldn't have to stay in a motel. I think she wanted me to see the two of them together, knowing that it would dispel any misgivings I had.

She was right. My father was acting like, well, a man in his early seventies. But he was a man in love all the same, a man showering affection on his housemate, often sitting with her on the couch holding hands, and not only supervising the food preparations, he was working together with her, side by side.

I'd never seen him do any of these things before. The division of domestic labour he and my mother had worked out had, in recent years, rarely brought them closer than 2 metres from one another unless they were at the dinner table.

With Georgie the body contact was close and it was constant. When my father sat down to eat, she would pause behind him for a moment before she sat down, her hands on his shoulders. They'd moved into my mother's larger bedroom, and were sleeping in the same bed, openly retiring for midday naps together, and they always returned smiling, usually holding hands.

She was caring for him with an attentiveness my mother long ago gave up on. For instance, my father owned a large sit-down lawn mower, and made a practice of perching the wheels atop the retaining wall at the far end of his lawn in order to cut the grass. Below the retaining wall was a steep slope that he'd tumbled down several times, and for years my mother had complained that he was going to go over the edge with the mower and kill himself.

The first time Georgie saw him perform this stunt, she complained about it, too: it *was* dangerous, and with his failing sight, it was only a matter of time before there was an accident. But she did more than complain. She bought a gas-powered weed whacker, and made a point of cranking it up and cutting all the grass along the retaining wall herself whenever he started the big mower, making sure she had it done before he got anywhere near the retaining wall. Surprisingly, he let her do it.

This, and dozens of other more mammalian courtesies they showed one another, were impossible not to buy into, and all of us did. I did drive down to the concrete bench by the walkway along Skaha Lake where my brother and sisters and I had paid for a commemorative plaque for my mother, and I sat on her bench and explained what was happening up on the hill to myself and to her. My explanation wasn't completely articulate, and it didn't take long:

life goes on, and when it is this sweet, no one has the right to reject it. And, well, here we all are in the world as it is . . .

It was her kind of logic, and I think she'd have accepted it.

*   *   *

The wedding was held at 5 p.m. in the seniors' centre not far down the hill from the house. The entire extended family was there, straggling in merrily from all over British Columbia. An hour before the ceremony my father called my brother and me into his study.

"How do I look?" he said, simply. It was a real question, because with his failing eyesight, he wasn't sure about the fine details. I looked him over, and noticed that parts of his face weren't properly shaven.

"You need to clean up your face a little," I said. "Where's your razor?"

"I have trouble shaving," he admitted. "Can you fix it for me? I want to look my best."

My brother retrieved the razor—an old electric one—and we took turns buzzing off the bits of his beard he'd missed. The skin on his cheeks was like parchment, and it reminded me of how old and fragile he'd become. I hadn't been in such close proximity to him since I was a small child, either physically or emotionally. I was fighting off tears by the time we had him cleaned up, and he spotted it.

"What the hell's the matter with you?" he said.

"Nothing," I answered. "It isn't every day your father gets married."

*   *   *

And then the wedding itself, ah yes. Was it splendid, a union of beauty and promise like his first wedding in 1936? No. But this groom and bride wanted it and one another as much as the bride and groom had 67 years before. It was a ceremony in which desire defeated halting speech and physical infirmity, where tenderness triumphed over sentimentality, where the bride and groom danced until midnight, not quite young but vigorous anyway, and then went home to perform acts of God knows what, but surely acts of love. It was, best of all, an event that not one wedding guest's cynicism withstood.

In the days and weeks and months that followed, there was domestic bliss in my father's house, and it was enriched by their sense that every moment was precious. Mortality didn't quite loom over their happiness, but it was there, palpable, and they embraced that along with the rest. The local newspaper got wind of them, and did a slightly malicious full-page spread on their "love life" without ever getting it clear, as no one in both slightly embarrassed families had, if there was a distinction between "love life" and sex.

They got just eight months. Then Georgie suffered a stroke in the same bed where my mother had hers three years before, and in virtually the same circumstances. My father, with his hearing aid out, didn't quite hear her attempts to rouse him, or decided that her muted thrashing about was a bad dream. He went back to sleep and by morning, the crucial hours for remedial measures had passed, and it was too late for recovery: Georgie was paralyzed on one side, her speech permanently gone, her cognition profoundly truncated.

Not so organized a woman as my mother, Georgie had no living will, and in fact, no contingency plans of any other kind. She'd been a woman prepared to take life as it came to her. Since it had brought her my father, she believed that not all the unexpected things in life were to be dreaded. And my father, in the time since my mother's death, had lost his phobias about illness and infirmity. He drove to the hospital with her in the ambulance, and in the weeks and months and years that followed, he was constantly by her side. He remained a daily visitor until her death, sitting with her for hours even though she was unable to speak or understand much of what he was saying. He held her hand, showered her with kisses, making the arduous drive to the hospital each day in his rickety old car, winter and summer, to visit his beloved. Not once did anyone hear him complain about it, either. "It gives me something to do," he said, without a trace of self-pity.

*   *   *

Did all this turn my father into a saint? Not hardly. He remained what he'd always been: a good man, but not quite a "nice" man. His grief over losing Georgie didn't make him lose track of the practicalities he lived by. A few months after the prognosis for her future was certain, he quietly cut her out of his will, and set out once again in search of companionship, even though he continued to spend time with her daily.

He lost his driver's licence when the local television station challenged him to a filmed driving test. They'd called him after he wrote a letter to the newspaper protesting that making him retest every year was "government meddling" and when he ran five stop signs while the camera was rolling and the station showed it on the nightly news, the Motor Vehicle Branch rescinded his privileges. He got the licence back by finally having a cataract removed, and it made him, well, a driving menace with partial vision in one eye. Within weeks of the operation he deployed the usual combination of charming guile and aggression to force the authorities to let him drive again. He had places to go, he said. People to meet.

My brother hired several live-in housekeepers to watch over him, but one after another they fled because he insisted on more than housekeeping: he could take care of himself, goddamn it to hell. What he wanted was physical affection, and he refused to live with anything less.

He continued to cultivate his garden, growing tomatoes, pruning the roses—and dousing them all with pesticides. He even trimmed the trees below the bank by himself as he always had, even though it was getting riskier each time out. When he grew agitated at a neighbour's refusal to trim a hedge that partly obscured his view of the city below the hill, he sniped at the poor man for months, and when that didn't work, he dumped several gallons of herbicide along the property line, turning the view-blocking hedge into a row of leafless twigs. The neighbour sued him, and my brother had to settle out of court without telling my father he'd bought the neighbour off. "Uncooperative sonofabitch," my father grumbled. "I'll do it again, if he replants them."

Several months after that, the neighbour decided he'd had enough of my father, and began to prepare his house for sale. Part of the prep involved repainting the backyard swimming pool, and I happened to be there while that was going on. The neighbour, an overweight man in his early sixties, was doing the repaint himself. He'd rented a paint compressor and spray gun for the job, and one afternoon while I was out in the yard, he started up the compressor, and as I watched, leaned over the pool to spray the sides and bottom. Within seconds, the device exploded in his hands, sending a cloud of white paint high into the air, and knocking the man backward. He lay there, not moving, for a long moment, stunned or injured—or for all I knew, dead. I was about to go to his aid, but before that, I wanted to tell my father to call an ambulance. He too had heard the compressor start, and was standing a few feet behind me—doubled over with laughter.

I turned back to the prostrate neighbour and saw that he was getting to his feet. He was wobbly, but apparently unharmed. I called out to him and asked if he was okay.

"I'm fine," he said. "The hose on this thing burst, that's all."

My father, by now, was standing beside me, grinning. "Serves the sonofabitch right," he said, loud enough for the neighbour to hear.

The next day, a few hours after my son Max arrived from Vancouver on the bus, my father asked us to change the bulbs on the strings of Christmas lights with which he'd always decorated his house. We cheerfully agreed to help out, and were soon clambering around the gently sloped roof exchanging old bulbs for the new ones he'd gone downtown and purchased before we arrived. At one point I happened to glance behind me and discovered that my father, by then 97 years old, had climbed the ladder and was standing directly behind us, teetering slightly, but clearly determined to make sure we did the job right.

"For God's sake, Dad," I said. "You shouldn't be up here."

"Don't tell me what to do," he snapped, glowering.

January 2008:
Blue Skies

---

*H*ARTLEY FAWCETT died a couple of months short of his 101st birthday in January 2008. He'd been a man who set his goals early on, achieved them by the age of 60, and then spent 40 years doing exactly and only what he damn well pleased. He was in relatively good health until two weeks before his death, and he knew where all the cards in his deck were until the last 48 hours. Through most of the last several decades of his life, he believed he possessed everything a sensible man could ask for, and when I look at the world through his eyes, I can see why he thought so. He was a lucky man, and he'd lived a happy life.

When such a life ends after a century, it isn't relevant, it seems to me, to mourn its end as if it is a tragedy. What the relevant responses are supposed to be, I'm not sure. The formal, polite gestures seem empty, and to tell the truth, I've experienced little regret since he died, even though I miss him and the cheerful wisdom he dispensed in the last few years of his run. I'm about equally likely to laugh or break into tears when I think about him.

My feelings about my father aren't what counts, despite our culture's insistence on me having them long, loud, 12-stage, and in public. What matters more—or ought to—is what I learn from his happiness, and what made him so happy at a point in his life when most elderly people are staring at the wall and remembering how much more fun life used to be. It seems to me that *not* attempting to uncover what made him a happy man would be foolish and dishonourable, particularly since he himself vastly preferred practical understanding to maudlin chest-pounding. What was this guy about?

My father's last seven years were his best, and maybe his happiest: he married for a second time, had innumerable other affectionate and occasionally erotic relationships with a startling assortment of people, and he became sweeter and more attentive of others the closer he got to the end. He also became conscious of and curious about these changes, and I think he'd be disappointed if I didn't at least try to figure out what changed him and what can be learned from it.

I see him every day when I look at the nine 5 x 7 photographs of him I've hung on the walls of my coach house writing/studio/library guest house in Toronto. In one of my two favourites, both of which are in the middle of this book, he's in his early forties, sitting on some boxes in a rail yard. He's wearing a dark three-piece suit, tie, and a snap-brim hat on his head that just covers his eyes. He's good looking in a square-jawed, square-shouldered way, and until you see how large his hands are—farmer's hands—you might think he's a dandy or a gangster. He wasn't. He was a family man and he was a salesman, and although I didn't understand it, he was equally passionate about both. My other favourite is the one where he's sitting on the motorcycle, looking tough. I grin every time I look at it, and then marvel at the distance he travelled from there to where he ended up.

What I see in both photos is that he was a good-looking man, better looking than I've ever been, even though we're built similarly, erect, broad-shouldered, tall enough. In his prime he stayed handsome in a heavy-set way, carrying about 200 pounds on his frame until he was in his late seventies, and he was as strong as an ox, able to scoop up small great-grandchildren and throw them over his shoulders when he was in his mid-nineties.

He had a very, very long prime, and an unusual one: seventy years at full speed. Into his nineties he was consistently taken for a man twenty years younger. The overwhelming impression he delivered to the world, from his youth to the very end, was that he was comfortable and engaged in a world he understood and felt on top of.

The most obvious source of my father's happiness, not surprisingly, was his good fortune: good looks, good health, the knack of making money, natural charm he could turn up and down to meet the situation, and no bad luck.

But his good fortune wasn't merely personal. He lived his entire life in western North America, the most stable part of the world during his century. There were no man-made disasters or military battles, and the worst natural disaster he witnessed personally was a 1948 river flood in Prince George, B.C., that did little more than drench the town in muddy water. Even there, the house he'd built was on a plateau well above the flood's reach. This wasn't luck. He'd have had it this way: it's okay to be a bystander, but only fools do their bystanding from the middle of a busy highway or on the banks of a river that floods every spring.

He believed that for a man to become a victim that man had to also be a fool. That's how he saw his life, and everyone else's. Given the sorts of things that happened to people during the twentieth century, those were the words of someone deeply, and maybe obliviously, fortunate.

Location was only one of the ways life blessed him. His placement in history was another. He came of age in the 1920s, and so missed the First World War, where military combat was the most psychologically destructive and physically lethal mass event human beings have ever consented to take part in. He then avoided military service in the Second World War without trying: he was in his thirties when the war started, married with children, had a job that was deemed necessary to the "war effort"—and characteristically, he didn't volunteer.

If he shirked danger, he didn't ever avoid hard work. He'd been able to get and keep his jobs throughout the Depression, managing to save enough to put a down payment on a house when he married. His postwar work ethic made him a moderately wealthy man, despite his lack of formal education. All of his offspring survived childhood and adolescence, and mostly inherited his good health while experiencing reasonable degrees of prosperity themselves. Another part of his luck was that he didn't outlive any of them.

He was lucky in other, less tangible ways. At the beginning of his life, he was the adored youngest son of a doting mother who breastfed him intermittently until he was almost seven years old. Whether that was a source of his lifelong good health is hard to calculate firmly; but it made him supremely comfortable in his skin the way people who know they're loved are, and the effects lasted a hundred years. He wasn't accident prone and he was never, as they say, in the wrong place at the wrong time. The worst injuries he suffered in his several auto accidents were minor cuts and bruises. This last item is a bigger deal than it sounds, since through his twenties he'd been a motorcyclist, and when he gave up his bike he spent two decades as a commercial traveller in landscapes with primitive roads and poorly maintained cars.

His mishaps remained minor as he grew old, but because he continued to do everything his own way, they gained a sometimes-delicious element of slapstick. He fell off roofs and walked away barely shaken up, he tumbled down steep embankments and crawled back up, ruffled but undamaged. This continued until, on his ninety-ninth birthday, he tumbled off a slippery porch, landing on a hefty roll of twenty-dollar bills he'd taken to keeping in his hip pocket instead of a wallet, and its bulk broke his hip. Even while he was near death in the weeks that followed the fall, he understood the irony of the accident and played it for the practical joke on him that it was. I think it was this laughter and his still-intact will that turned what should have been a life-ender into a good time within a few months, and then he rode it for nearly two years. Once he was institutionalized, he accepted it without complaint, and used his completely intact charm to make himself the institution's favourite patient/resident. Smart guy.

Life gave him some breaks, yes. Yet on a thousand occasions, his wilfulness and practical intelligence gave those breaks the shove that transforms here-now-gone-tomorrow luck into accumulative good fortune. A man in the right place at the right time he may have been, but he always made that into more than life's slippery surfaces give for free. He was always the first one to put his shoulder to the wheel, and he was frugal and very shrewd, both in his business decisions and his judgment of people and situations. That's probably why the opportunities kept rolling almost to the end, when he stopped caring about them and got interested in other things.

Until he was well into his nineties, I didn't, any more than he did, think about whether he was happy, or about what sorts of materials his personal happiness was constructed from. I was the rebellious youngest son of a rebellious youngest son, and while I was butting heads with him, it seemed like what I was born to do. But it meant that he and I wasted nearly all of our time together with nose-to-nose stare-downs and contests of will, neither of us able to see or appreciate the other beyond the uneven conflict of two alpha males. The things that appeared to give him the most pleasure were making money and telling everyone around him what to do and what was right and wrong, and I curled my lip at all of it. Since I was the weaker alpha I did my best to keep some distance between us, but when I couldn't sidestep him I fought back against both his authority and his influence with more ferocity than I've shown in any other part of my life. Our battles were loud and ferocious, and when I was younger, sometimes they got physical.

But by the time he was into his last decade, our fights were less intense and frequent, maybe because our stupid war no longer compelled either of us. He was, I think, growing tired of fighting with me. And while I'd learned how to win battles against him, I'd realized that I was never going to win the war—which is to say, he wasn't ever going to see me as I wanted to be seen. As his nineties began there was a cold and wary armistice between us, and then, after my mother died, the war simply ended, because, well, he changed. Oh, sure, I let go, too, a little. It was impossible not to admire his courage and resourcefulness, and his growing sweetness made it possible to forget what an overbearing shithead he'd been for so many years.

In his last five years, I started to enjoy his company for the first time in my adult life, and when that happened, I regretted that I hadn't found ways to get along with him when he was younger, and wondered how I could find out what he knew about the world before he wasn't around to talk to. It wasn't just me breaking with the toxic past, either. He'd begun to ask questions of me and other family members we never dreamed he'd ask: What did we think about things? What did we feel?

Yet for all the changes, he was exactly who he'd always been. He continued to feud with his neighbours, still proselytized Barley Max to anyone who'd listen, and he still called fools what they were whenever he spotted them. And he still cheated at cards, and now sometimes at chess I'd catch him moving his pieces to better positions when his opponents weren't paying attention. He'd probably always done this, but now he didn't try to suppress the giggle when he did it.

But as far as he was capable, he became a listener. This wasn't easy, since he was seriously deaf. But he listened to everyone—unless he was calling you on the cellphone my brother got for him, which he couldn't hear anything on. When he called you on the cellphone, you listened, and he talked. But face-to-face, he listened attentively to the answers to the many questions he asked us. He and I began to talk, tentatively at first, but gradually, with increased openness. After he went into the rest home, the openness grew, and the dozen or so long conversations we had there were wide-ranging and affectionate. And yet even here, he remained himself. He bumped the dozier patients out of the way with his motorized wheelchair in the corridors, pretended he was going to put cutlery into the open mouths of the several slack-jawed stroke victims in the facility when he found them sleeping in the common room with their mouths open, and he remained irreverent about the misfortunes and vulnerabilities of the people around him—and his own.

He survived 21 months after he broke his hip. A few months after he was settled in the extended care facility, Georgie, who was in another wing of the same facility, and whom he visited each afternoon, wending his way down the hallways in his wheelchair, died. He was sad, but philosophical about it. There had been, he said, not much left of her at the end. As his second summer in extended care wound down, he lost a girlfriend he'd liked enough that the two of them, six weeks after his hundredth birthday, were busted while climbing into bed together without a stitch of clothing on. After the girlfriend died, he seemed to lose some of his drive, and he started to talk, between the increasingly gentle soliloquies he delivered to anyone who visited, about being tired.

"How the hell do I get out of this life?" he asked me the last time I visited him.

I told him that I didn't know, and left the question hanging without offering him any idiotic clichés about it being okay to let go. I preferred it the way he'd put it several months before that, when I asked him how he was doing and he recognized that I wanted the truth.

"Not so good," he'd said. "I can't hear, I can't see much, and I have to wear diapers most of the time. I'm not really having much fun at all." Then he paused, as he'd taken to doing, giving himself time to calculate the greater truth of whatever he was pondering. "But you know," he concluded, "this is still a hell of a lot more fun than being six feet under the ground."

When I first visited after he went into the extended care facility, he keyed a lot of our conversations with what I thought was a rhetorical question: "How in hell did I get this old?"

It was a real question to him, and he was honestly bewildered about the answer. Because there *was* no standard answer, he used it as a springboard for stories about his past, many of which I'd never heard before, and which he recounted as if he were himself hearing them for the first time. He seemed to be testing their truth, searching them for insights he'd have never entertained a decade before even if they'd clubbed him over the head.

When I visited him close to Thanksgiving after his first summer in the facility and found him sporting a deep suntan, he explained that he sat outside most days, even after the air began to grow cool in September. "I like to feel the sunlight on my skin," he said, when I asked him what it was about.

There was that familiar pause as he thought over the implications of his most recent thought. "You know," he said after a moment, "I built five houses in my life, and not a goddamned one of them had a place where you could sit in the sun." Another pause, as he thought *this* over. He smiled, not quite ruefully, as he settled in around the interesting new thing he'd uncovered about himself. "I guess my mind was on other things."

He wasn't accusing himself of negligence, just plating a recognition that was interesting to both of us: perspective changes with focus, not just with age. There were many more similar insights, but there was no self-pity, no self-stroking, and few regrets. He was, simply, interested. He was exploring parts of himself and his experience he'd ignored for almost a century, and it was time to understand it and himself.

As Remembrance Day approached in his last autumn, he began thinking over the John McCrae poem "In Flanders Fields," which he'd always liked but now decided he ought to memorize as a way of, as he put it, keeping his mind from getting stale. I think he was circling the last verse of the poem and its fuzzy ideas about passing the torch from the dead to the living—looking, as he'd always done, for the slogans and formulae. But when I talked to him on the phone a few days after November 11, he said that he'd decided he liked the first two verses best. He talked for several minutes about "those poor boys" who'd died in the First and Second World Wars, and how stupid the government was to be again sending young men not much different "to get their asses shot off in some godforsaken shithole."

He was up to other things, too, one of them complicated and momentous. He decided to change his will to leave his estate, the bulk of which he'd long since dispersed to my siblings and I via tax loopholes, to his grandchildren. He'd realized that his children weren't exactly suffering financially, and that he could do a good turn to everyone by leaving what he had left to the next generation. Here, as seemed the case generally over the last several years, it wasn't ego that moved him. This was the fruit of his improved powers of domestic observation, and it carried a predictably strong element of common sense. I suspected he'd been rethinking the power of parental wealth to control and corrupt children—something he'd employed, or tried to, with us. But now he decided to take some of that corrupting power away from us, while (not incidentally, in his mind) saving us from having to pay taxes on the money we did transfer to our children. A week after he signed the new will, pneumonia, the old person's friend, set in, and he began to spiral downward.

I got the call to come five days before the end and I was there for the last 36 hours of his life. My sister Serena had arrived a day earlier to relieve Ron, who'd stayed with him until it became too painful for him to witness. When I arrived my sister told me he'd lost consciousness a few hours before my plane touched down, and that the doctor didn't think he'd regain consciousness. I can't say for sure that he knew that two of his children were with him, but he did grip my hand firmly enough to let me know he was aware that he wasn't alone. Good enough. This was his show, and companionship was what he really wanted: being alone had been the one thing in life he'd found difficult to bear.

He had a hard death even though he'd been at peace with the idea of dying. He—or maybe it was life itself—hung on more than 24 hours after there was no reason to expect he could, or that he wanted to. Serena and I held his still-huge but lifeless hands for hours on end during that painful day, watching his lined face collapse and become, in the last 12 hours, the fretful face of an infant entangled in troubled dreams—remembering his century-ago passage into the world, or hesitating before the one he was about to enter now.

Death, as I'd learned from watching my mother die, doesn't offer Hollywood comforts to the dying: no theme music in the background, no slo-mo Defining Moments, no backlit tableaux. There did seem, with both my parents, a point at which their conscious will dissolved and the darkness poured into their minds and bodies, unhurriedly and almost casually, without permitting either of them a shred of dignity as they departed.

Witnessing my father's final descent brought back my mother's more difficult death eight years before. Hers had been a death that hadn't exactly been infused with conventional grief, either. She'd been "only" 90, but like my father, she'd been prepared to die, albeit in a different way. Both of them had orchestrated their deaths on their own terms, and both died without regrets, which is about as good as it gets. But "peaceful" wasn't what came to mind for what I witnessed, either time. It was painful, raw, and humiliating, and the only illumination it came with was from the fluorescent tubes in the ceiling. I learned nothing from or about death, except its arrogance and its power, and that it wins, always.

Yet for all its implacable absoluteness, death opens its witnesses to life. In the several years that followed my mother's death, I opened up to the nuances in my father's character I'd been missing, seeing things about him that interested me in spite of myself. Most of them contradicted the fury of our father-son conflict.

I hadn't, for instance, understood his frankly merry resistance to all forms of bullshit—except his own, to which he remained oblivious until the end. He'd always been able to see through other people with effortless clarity, maybe because he had utterly unsentimental instincts about human motives that stopped just this side of cynicism. When he was younger, he could price any man's suit a mile off, though he wore nothing but the cheapest suits himself. I'd grown up watching him gleefully cut visiting business executives down to size without them quite seeing how he did it. Now, remembering it made me laugh out loud. And I thought about that sixth sense he had about hostile intentions, and how he always nailed attackers when they were still in the windup. Except, I now recognized, me. I'd landed more than a few on him over the years that must have cut him to the core, and he'd taken them, every time, without retaliating.

Another thing I hadn't appreciated near enough was his casual but profound industriousness. He got things done even when all he had on his to-do list was growing African violets to sell at the local hospital auxiliary booth. As he was heading into his late nineties, he remained perpetually busy and engaged, wrestling with problems that were how-to one moment, abstract the next. I think he was happiest when whatever he had on his mental workbench contained elements of both.

When I thought through this industriousness, I began to recognize that a quirky mix of the practical and the quixotic had always been present in whatever he did, and I recalled, from my childhood, that even during the years when he was working 14 hours a day building his business, he'd found time to plant gardens each year, including setting down a brace of rose bushes that he ordered after Christmas from the Sears catalogue, none of which ever survived the following winter. It was a ridiculous sort of stubbornness to do this year after year, but it was only part of the story. He also planted, together with my mother, those large, sensible, and productive vegetable gardens. He did most of the bull work, and he did it with so little fanfare that none of us really remembered he'd done anything at all until he had us filling gunnysacks with potatoes in September. After he moved to Penticton he'd gardened pretty much the same way until he broke his hip—except that now the roses survived the winters, and the tomatoes he'd always wanted to grow could thrive.

Until close to the end he took walks most days, accompanied by the two small mutts my sisters had given him before my mother died. The last of these dogs disappeared over the edge of his lawn in the mouth of a coyote about eight months before he broke his hip. He was heartbroken about it, but there was more than mere sadness. There was the new thoughtfulness, and a tinge of resignation that carried no trace of self-pity.

"Life can be very cruel," he said, and then, before passing judgment on its cosmological significance, took the now-familiar pause. "I did have many hours of joy from those little dogs, so I have no regrets."

When I was cleaning out his house after the funeral, I found dozens of contraptions he'd invented over the years, nearly all of them created to accomplish some task no one but he would have bothered with—a spidery soaking device soldered from long fingers of 3/8th-inch copper tubing so he could water five or six of his African violet clones at the same time without getting water on the leaves; a 500-gallon steel tank in his basement designed to catch and store rainwater; or a small electric fan screwed to a custom-welded base at an oblique angle to ventilate or dry God only knows what. He had a brain that was in gear from the moment of waking in the morning until he parked it at night. And yet he was more than an unreflecting productivity machine. He had a lifelong gift for thinking on the fly, and he thought about *everything* with the same vigour and curiosity until a few days before his death.

It reminded me that until I was six or seven years old, I lived in a house that had pinball machines and jukeboxes in the front hallway—which he rigged so we could play them for free. Among the pleasures of my early childhood was sitting in front of those beautiful 1940s Wurlitzers with their columns of cascading lights, punching in selections at random so I could watch the intricate armature pick up the disks, lift them onto the turntable, and set the needle into the groove. I must have listened to the music, too, because I still have a thousand late forties and early fifties tunes stored in my head, tunes that I often find myself humming for no reason. My father was building the financial nest egg with which he bought his first business, but I was acquiring, along with the music of an era, a lifelong fascination with mechanical contraptions. I have the same fascination for pre-electronic pinball machines, and I know more about now-obsolete mechanical coin exchange devices than a sane man should. I suspect my insistence on understanding human systems has its roots in that same period: everything, my father taught me, is a device, and devices can always be tinkered with, made to work better. I don't think I'd have ever written a book without that lesson.

The one thing he and I didn't ever talk about during his last years was the state of hostility that had existed between us for most of my life and for nearly 50 years of his. It seemed, I guess, prudent to both of us to let that sleeping dog lie. But in the hours immediately before his death, I found myself wondering exactly why, from about the time I reached adolescence, we'd disagreed over virtually everything except maybe the colour of the sky.

That's when I realized that we'd disagreed on that, too. *It*, I now realized, was the root disagreement that had precipitated most of the others.

My father, you see, fervently believed that the sky was always blue. Clouds were temporary things, and behind them, the sky was always clear. I believed just as passionately that the sky was constructed of other, darker colours. For him the blue derived from the openness of his vista: what he perceived, always, was a world of opportunities, a realm with few shadows and no dark nights at all. And me? I wasn't about to let his perpetual optimism trample me or science. I insisted that the blueness of the sky was light reflecting from dust particles in the atmosphere, and that once you got to the edge of space it was jet black. I splattered clouds and darkness across his permanent daylight whenever we clashed.

The fact was this: when I thought over what he believed about the world and how a man ought to conduct himself in it, he'd just plain seemed *wrong*. Above my cloudy horizons were squadrons of bombers loaded with nuclear weapons, always minutes from fail-safe. The hills he found so picturesque for me were filled with missile silos, and the streets and podiums were filled with fast-talking bullshitters who refused to acknowledge any of it.

It didn't matter to me that my father's actions were often sincerely aimed at serving what he thought were my best interests. He was rushing toward the future and I was intent on preventing it from happening. Even his concern for my welfare had always felt like a moral undertow that would drag me into his zone of control if I relaxed. I had to do things differently, see, and if I didn't, my balls would shrivel up and drop off and the screwed-up world would continue to fall apart—or it would end in a gargantuan ball of fire that would consume everything and everyone I loved.

It never occurred to me that my father truly, sincerely believed the sky was fundamentally blue—and growing bluer. Nor did I understand how deeply I believed that it was grey and fading to black.

In my father's youth, and into the era that lasted well into his prime, most things belonged to men much like him. They had earned what they had by struggling through economic ruin and privation during the Depression, then by winning an epic war against the evil of Nazi-Fascism. They felt sure—correctly, as it turned out—that the initiative-sapping global evil of Soviet Communism would also be defeated. He, and men like him, could reasonably expect their lives to get progressively better, collectively and individually, particularly if they were able to make and carry out practical, businesslike plans. Their sky really *was* blue.

My generation, the one born during and immediately after the Second World War, has experienced the world very differently. We haven't had to face privation or social upheaval, and, in Canada at least, we have fought no wars, heroic or otherwise. But as children, we were subjected to a political system and its educational apparatus that taught us that an unthinkably violent and destructive war was a strong probability, and that it might be inevitable. For a few years this system had us regularly crouching beneath our school desks while air-raid sirens wailed through the hallways. These drills were designed to prepare us to survive the blast of a nuclear weapon, but we understood in our bones that if an attack came we wouldn't survive, and that it would be the end of everything.

I can't speak for all of my contemporaries, but I can testify that this twisted my outlook on human possibilities and human motives. It convinced me, first, that human beings are fundamentally unreliable and possibly crazy—how else could the most able of them devise a future so bleak and dangerous. It also infected the way I've been able to think of the future, then and since. Bouncing around inside my brain is a nine-year-old who once crouched under his school desk, and this child still thinks that he was supposed to get blown up by the crazy people who run the world, and that there isn't supposed to *be* a future.

Now, that future didn't come about, although the evidential proofs of humanity's self-destructive madness have continued to pile up. We're now a decade into the twenty-first century, and the nuclear nightmare has receded to the point where the worst that's likely to happen in my lifetime is that one or two cities will be obliterated by suicidal religious zealots detonating suitcase nukes obtained either from the Russian Mafia or constructed from materials sold by some profit-focused corporation in our midst.

That same nine-year-old got it tangled up inside his head, not so surprisingly, that his father was part and parcel of the coming end of the world, because his father was the only one he saw who made things happen. And since a head tangled in childhood can almost never be completely disentangled, not by facts, futures, therapies, or human kindness, the deeds and the underlying life manual of this child's father became permanently suspect. These are the ridiculous reasons the sky was never quite blue for me, and why even getting it to overcast, given the radioactive universe of blackened cinders I once believed was our collective fate, is difficult.

I'm not whining about this, be clear. I've had a good and easy life, and part of the reason is my father's hard-working industriousness, which has made it possible for me to work as an independent freelance writer for long periods of my life rather than scuffling at a nine-to-five job. Still, seeing shadows is a fact of the way I see things, one that I share, to greater or lesser degree, with a lot more of my baby-boomer contemporaries than is generally credited. We're *just not optimists*, and unless we're really thick between the cultural ears, we don't see the future as an unlimited vista of glorious opportunities. We dread the future, whatever else we're saying about it or doing with it.

I'm not merely recording "feelings" here, either. As early as the 1970s, the moral high ground was shifting away from North America, going global. It would not much longer belong to white people, and especially not to white men like me, who have, since the Second World War ended, become the first-resort enemy of everything and everyone virtuous. We're the fat cats trying to hold the lid down against what is good and just.

That's why, with no élan and a belief in the inevitable nuclear winter indelibly etched in our subconscious minds, many young men like me passed on big and blue skies, turned our backs on black and white for grey, and gave up on initiative itself. We understand that even the most basic opportunity requires us to exploit other people and their environments, and with ecological and economic decline visible and accelerating, we haven't been decently able to even desire our personal conditions to get better, not on the terms the prevailing politics and economics offer. Big plans have resulted in big catastrophes, and so our instinct is not to make plans *at all*. We live, instead, from private gratifications to small pleasures, and we try not to make the world worse than it has become.

But look, it isn't all bad. The skies—and I do remind myself of this from time to time—are grey, not black and filled with lethal isotopes. This is a world with many positives: civil and human rights have been widely extended, we now treat women almost as well as heterosexual male forklift drivers; homosexual normality is almost accepted; animals are treated better; and a lot of people in the developed world have become sensitized about the degree to which we're making our planet uninhabitable. See how this works? Even when I'm up, I'm pointing down.

While my father was dying it happened that I was reading a book of essays titled *Stardust* by Bruce Serafin, a Vancouver writer of great intelligence and sensitivity, but one saddled with a cultural pessimism even more extreme than mine. I'd known Bruce personally and had admired him for many years, and it had struck me as tragic when he died, six months before my father began his spiral out of the world, of cancer. He'd been just 57, and he died with a full intellectual agenda yet to be carried out. His shy, obtuse and utterly given-to-second-thoughts nature made him as unlike my father as a human being could get.

The essay I read and reread over that 24 hours while my father hung on to life concerned the novel *Underworld*, by the American novelist Don DeLillo. DeLillo's novel is ostensibly a virtuoso regression in American time from the present to the moment of Bobby Thompson's famous home run that decided the 1951 National League baseball pennant race and which, in DeLillo's view, was the last completely bright and heroic event in American history.

DeLillo's book is actually about the gradual darkening and descent of the psychological currents that made up cultural reality in the last half of the twentieth century in America. What Serafin spotted in *Underworld* was the degree to which that darkening has come to be seen as natural and without alternatives.

The thought that came to me as I read Serafin's essay and watched my father dying was this: for my father, that underworld, which occupies large elements of my conscious and unconscious attention, simply didn't exist. He would have found DeLillo's depiction of American life utterly incomprehensible. "Underworld?" I could almost hear him say. "What the hell is that?"

In the *Stardust* essay, Serafin argued that the underworld is the strange sort of virtual simultaneity of things that has supplanted linear history and "progress" in contemporary social and psychological cognition. Ramped up by the immense penetrating power of modern mass media, past and future have been crowded out, leaving everyone and everything in a claustrophobic, juiced-up here-and-now, with history and the future converging on each instant as either a threat or an unwanted seduction instead of aspiration and hope.

Serafin argued that we're marching not to a bright future, but toward an oppressive totality where individual experience and initiative have been invaded and corrupted by media: inside its totality, the Kennedy brothers were assassinated yesterday and will be again tomorrow, the space shuttle will explode again and again inside our minds because we've had the lurid film-at-five forced on us by television over a hundred yesterdays and we can watch it again tomorrow on YouTube. Everything exists in this totality now, fused cognitively and culturally by the implosion of fact and ideology. And inside the totality, meaning can't exist for more than a few minutes before it is rendered obsolete by an onslaught of contradictory data. That's the underworld: the shadow that accompanies this fusion/implosion where nothing can remain exact and particular.

Memory and cognition here are never quite free of the violence of our parents and ancestors, and the future, well, that belongs to everyone but us. The Underworld, then, is the collective burden of guilt that tries to convince us that our lives, present and future, are the sum total of the bad or thoughtless deeds of the past, carried on a wearied and stressed-out suspicion that politics and social life—and perhaps even one's private thoughts—are manipulated by remote corporations, government agencies, the mob, even space aliens. Sanity begins, as it must in such a world, to collapse into an emotionalized matrix that is perpetually clouded.

I sat in the darkened palliative care room my father was dying in and tried to come up with a definition of the Underworld that he would understand. Finally, it came to me: I would get him to imagine a world where you couldn't make plans.

In my head I heard his voice repeating what I'd heard from him a hundred times: "You've got to have plans. If you don't make plans you can't achieve anything. I had a plan all my life. I always knew where I was going in the big picture. Every single morning of my life I woke up and made my plan for that day, and then I carried it out. That's the only way to succeed at anything."

Then his other voice, the more gentle one from the last years, broke in: "How the hell do you think I got the energy to live a hundred years?"

That's when I remembered that for him, everything hadn't exactly been perfect. He hadn't been content with his marriage—his first one, anyway—a lot of people hadn't liked him for the way he spoke his mind, and by his own anecdotal accounting, the everyday world was full of jackasses, and politics and business were overrun with blowhards and crooks. I considered pointing out to him that just possibly things *were* getting worse, that there were more crooks and jackasses than in the past and that—

I stopped myself. Why would I do such a thing? Even if I made my point, he'd come up with a thousand instances of how things were terrific, that people were hard-working, and we'd be back arguing over what colour the sky was.

So in that deathbed room, I stopped this imaginary conversation. The only way I could make him understand my life was to blacken his blue sky, convince him that his life and his goals were illusions. So I pulled back, and I sat in the darkness with him as his companion. I said nothing, not even in my own mind. He was my father and I loved him—at that moment, as uncritically as I had since I was a small child. I loved him partly because I was duty-bound to it, but also because I loved what he'd become. He was remarkable: a man who'd taught himself, in his mid-nineties, almost deaf and nearly blind, how to care about other people in dozens of new ways. His vision of life had become sweeter and more encompassing than anything I had, and he deserved to die with it unchallenged. And that's how, agonized, struggling to draw one more breath, his eyes and cheeks caved in, his big-boned arms like his hands, seemingly too large for his body, my father died beneath his big blue sky.

One more thing. I've spent a fair amount of time since he died bemusedly coming to terms with the idea that elements of my character—my irascibility, my tendency to complain loudly but never more than half-seriously that the world seems to be full-to-the-brim with morons and self-serving irresponsible jackasses—are traits I inherited from him. It's as if, freed by his death, they've come clambering out of their hiding places in me, thus giving him exactly the kind of immortality he'd find most entertaining.

Most of these still-evolving traits, I'm aware, are also in part my private adaptations to the collapse of autocratic patriarchy, to the socially psychopathic evolution of entrepreneurial ethics, and other elements of the constellation of societal changes that have landed me in a world as a man with more than my share of alpha-male testosterone, but with no safe place for it to go except out the exhaust vent.

So be it. I've never, as I've already said, wanted to *be* my father or live my life as he did. His definition of maleness and authority are done, and even if my world is without substitutes and transformatives other than "no," I like it better than his. I like being no better or worse than anyone else, and I couldn't accept the privileges and presumptions his generation had even if I wanted them, which I don't. So what if most days I feel more like a sabre-toothed tiger than a man with a mission or that, like the overspecialized sabre-toothed tiger, I'm dressed to kill, but have nowhere to go but the bone-pile?

Then, just before I'm corrupted by the high/serious portends of this metaphor, I hear his cackle of laughter, identify it as not his at all, but my own, and feel the sky lighten above me.

Drowning

*F*IVE WEEKS AFTER my father's funeral I flew to Mexico with Leanna and Hartlea for the wedding of my elder son, Jesse, at the seaside village of Troncones, on Mexico's west coast. I was still getting used to the absurd idea that I was now at once an orphan and a patriarch, so the break was welcome for several reasons: I could practise looking dignified as a father of the groom, soak up some sun, do some thinking about the marriage of one's children and about my father's death, and ponder my own mortality.

Almost 20 years had gone by since I've spent any time on the coastal Pacific, and this was the first time I'd *ever* been in its tropics. While Jesse and his younger brother, Max, were kids I took them to B.C.'s Gabriola Island for parts of every summer—16 summers in all. In that part of the Pacific—the inside passage between Vancouver Island and the mainland—the sea is much calmer and colder, but somehow the feel and the aromas of the Troncones foreshore were recognizable, and the green water of the Pacific, so different from the blue Atlantic, was comfortingly familiar. How different could the rest of it be?

Before I left Toronto, I'd bought myself something I'd wanted for years but was never quite able to come to terms with the luxury of: a diving mask with prescription lenses. I'm a nearsighted and lazy snorkeller, you see. In the Gabriola days, my favourite way of snorkelling was to lie in about 25 centimetres of water while I examined the rich microecology of the Gulf Islands' sheltered sandstone pools. I've never been a particularly strong swimmer, and I arrived in Mexico 35 pounds overweight, out of shape, and in trouble with my lungs, which haven't responded happily to all the fresh air they're getting after 30 years of cigarette smoking. All those summers by the ocean turned Jesse to more adventurous water sports than myopic snorkelling. He became a surfer, and the wedding was being held, not surprisingly, given the extreme passion of surfers, not far from one of the best surfing beaches in Mexico. This should have been my first tip.

It didn't penetrate because Jesse, wishing to get everyone out to his out-of-the-way wedding location, described Troncones as a place where all things aquatic were safely possible: scuba diving, snorkelling, body and serious surfing. He'd cautioned me, sort of, that I should watch out for the undertow, adding that the surfers often had to rescue people from it, and that (by the way) a half-dozen fools drown along this stretch of coast each year. But hey, just use your common sense and you won't have a care. I assumed that the fools he was referring to were feckless surfers, who have a noticeably higher-than-normal mortality rate because of the inherent hazards of the sport. And common sense was easy, right?

I knew the Pacific Ocean and I understood my limits in the water.

Going snorkelling wasn't exactly my first priority at Troncones, and I postponed it until I'd been there five days out of sheer inertia. I might have put it off altogether except that I mentioned it to my nephew Jason, also there for the wedding, and he said he'd like to go out with me. So it was on the day of the wedding, about three hours before the ceremony was to commence, that the two of us finally strolled out to the south edge of Troncones's Manzanillo Bay, struggled into our flippers and masks and backed clownishly out into the surf. We'd agreed on a half-assed sort of plan: swim out along the rocky edge of the surfing spot, the shallows of which were said to be infested with sea urchins, nasty little beasts covered with poisonous spines. Jesse cautioned us to give them a wide berth.

I should have been checklisting the fairly long list of things that could go wrong as I backed out into the water, but my new mask didn't fit properly, and each time I submerged to test the seal, it flooded. Each time, I sputtered up, resettled the mask, and pushed out again. Eventually, I got it to co-operate, but the seal wasn't perfect. The mask continued to leak just enough that every 20 or 30 metres I had to stop to clear it. Before I'd even gotten comfortable in the water, Jason and I were 200 metres from the beach, if not very far from the rocky surfing shoreline we were supposed to stay clear of, and in about 3 or 4 metres of turbid, churning sea water. Below me—hugging the bottom—I could see the colourful foreshore fauna I was there to mingle with.

These fish didn't seem at all interested in mingling with me. They were busy keeping themselves from being crushed against the rocks by the surf or being picked off by the pelicans should they stray anywhere near the surface. Here again, I wasn't quite paying attention: I was waiting to see the fish, as I was used to, dallying playfully a few centimetres away, but the only way that was going to happen was if I dived down to their level and got kissy-face with them. That's what I did, despite the poor seal in the mask, which had to be cleared and resettled each time I surfaced.

After three or four of these dives, I began to perceive, dimly, that this really wasn't at all the relaxing sort of snorkelling I was used to, but that I'd been ignoring the arduousness of it because the corrective lenses were allowing me to see so much better. Now I began to recognize the presence of some things the corrective lenses didn't help with: strong tidal currents, timid fish, water that was filled with debris, and—this was the important datum—that I was beginning to tire.

I was, in physiological reality, doing everything possible to starve my body of oxygen: diving in the rough water and holding my breath, not breathing normally as I cleared the mask and snorkel when I surfaced, getting irritable with the poor viewing conditions and—hey!—those bloody seas are really rough. My only sensible moves were to notice these things when I did, and to signal to Jason, who was farther out and in no trouble, that I wanted—needed?—to head back in.

This is where the serious stuff got going. Getting out 200 metres from shore had been easy—far too easy, now that I thought about it. That meant that getting back to shore might not be easy at all. I tested this provisional theory for 20 or 30 seconds, and found its fault: not only was it not easy, it wasn't happening.

Uh-oh, I thought. What the hell is going on here? I swam toward shore for several more minutes, putting more effort into it, before a second theory emerged: this might be the undertow Jesse warned me about. It wasn't the fun kind of undertow I was expecting, the tug-at-your-ankles type I'd experienced a couple of times in the mild surf of the Caribbean. This was a more powerful and less entertaining drag-your-ass-out-to-sea kind of undertow.

I turned around to locate Jason—and as I did, immersed the snorkel tip and sucked a large mouthful of salty water into my lungs. I blew as much of it out as I could, cleared the snorkel, then the mask, turned back to the water, and began to chug my way toward the shore with still more determination. Panic? Not me.

When I looked up again, I still hadn't made any detectable progress—except maybe to increase the distance from the rocky surfing shoreline with its poison-spined sea urchins. Now there was something new and more alarming: buoyancy was becoming a difficulty. I wasn't just being pulled *out* to sea, I was being pulled *down*. For a few seconds, my brain could find nothing by which to process this: it continued to believe that I could float if I needed to, just like I'd always been able to, and anyway, wasn't I wearing flippers, which had, at least up to this moment in my life . . .

And off my brain went on that: *my life*, which might be just a few minutes from its end, because, hey, I was now sucking air, my lungs labouring to make up the oxygen already lost, my lungs which weren't working as efficiently as they used to, and which inefficiency, I, jackass that I am, hadn't added to the calculations, and my arms and my suddenly sinking legs, already leaden with lactic acid, weren't co-operating, and wait a minute, where *is* Jason? And why won't this mask stop filling with water? And what should I do now? Turn over on my back and swim that way? No, if I do that the snorkel tip goes into the water. Fine, then I'll dump it and the mask—and with it the expensive prescription lenses? Oh right, save the $300 and lose your life, idiot, and wait! You *know* what this is! *This* is panic, the one thing you can't do right now, because panic is what drowns people, so get a grip on yourself and tell Jason what you've figured out.

"Hey," I shouted as loudly as I can. *"I'm in trouble!"*

It was a real decision point, the kind you have to make in a split second and then live (or die) by it: *your ego or your life, dipstick*. But inside the interval of the decision I jetted into a darker present than I could remember inhabiting, *ever*, and as I did, a very strange thought emerged: *Hey! Why not let go? Why not drown? Who the hell cares, really? It's just you, not all the rest of the world, and the world will get over you soon enough.*

Before I could fully process this absolutely-in-my-entire-life-unprecedented proposition, I felt Jason's hand on my shoulder, and heard him asking me if I was okay. I admitted the truth: no, I'm in trouble, and—now extracted from that strangely abstract present—can you wave at the surfers, they'll come over, recalling Jesse's remark earlier, now registering accurately, that they rescue *swimmers*, and know what to do.

Jason let go of my shoulder, and I saw him signalling to a group of surfers 100 metres off—*is he in trouble, too?* No, it turned out later he was just anxious, both about me and maybe just a little about how hard it was getting back to shore, which he'd noticed, too. Also distracting him at the moment of crisis was that he'd recognized how much I resembled his grandfather/my father, recalling a moment from his childhood where he'd been in a swimming pool with him and now saw his grandfather as me, or me as him.

I dismissed the question of how Jason was doing because the answer to my *"Why not just drown?"* question arrived, and with convincing force: *No, you nitwit, you can't drown. It's your son's wedding day, and if you drown, he can't have the wedding, and how will that make you feel, you selfish numbskull?!*

Armed with this insight, I kept struggling toward shore, with that other voice, much softer now but even more seductive, murmuring, *"Hey, let go. Just drown. It's okay,"* the earlier panic now supplanted by an almost-entertaining sense of detachment and by the giggle-inducing thought that I wouldn't feel anything if I did drown. Then I began to hear the wheeze in my lungs become an interestingly alien rasp, and sensation in my legs ceased to feel like concrete and morphed into lead. There was a moment when this threatened to get the upper hand, and I almost stopped swimming.

But that other voice, the irritable remnant of me I recognized as my mother's coolness in emergencies, grew more intense with its scolding: *Oh, for Christ's sake, how could you have gotten into a mess like this on* this *day?!*

And then I heard Jason's voice break into the inner dialogue, hollering in my ear that he'd gotten the attention of a surfer, that he was on his way. *Hmm*, I thought, almost regretfully. *My trip into the infinite present that precedes oblivion is about to be interrupted. I'm going to survive. I'm not going to drown.*

It occurred to me later that day that, along with Jason and the surfer, it was *shame* and not will that saved me from drowning. That's interesting in a counter–Ayn Rand sort of way, I suppose. But in the practical world, the relevant item was that I *didn't* drown, and not only did I not drown, I didn't even have to bear the humiliation of being resuscitated on the beach by some surfer while he admonished me for being a gringo idiot. The surfer who came to rescue me didn't give me the hairy eyeball as he lifted me onto his board and paddled easily to shore. He just did it, like it was an everyday sort of thing; a job. Or better, indifferent courtesy.

And so I relaxed atop the board, detachedly listening to the harsh rasp of my breathing, and noting, the same way, how hard my heart was pounding. Was I about to have a heart attack? *"Hey,"* the soft voice said. *"That would be okay, too."*

No, it wouldn't. By the time the surfer touched solid ground and dumped me off the board, my heart rate had slowed, and my lungs had stopped shouting about the bad treatment they'd been given. I walked out of the water unassisted, and I even had enough presence of mind to thank my rescuer. He shrugged, and turned back toward the water unmoved: gringo idiots.

I sat down on the sand for several minutes to collect myself, wanting to go over that *"Why not drown?"* voice before it faded. I wasn't sure that I'd just experienced one of the profound moments in my life, but it *was* a unique one. Was this the genetic heritage of my Suffolk coastguardsmen ancestors kicking in, the ones who'd given my mother's family their fearlessness in the face of extinction?

Jason sat down beside me, but we had little to say to one another despite the permanent bond I sensed had been forged between us. We sat there for a few moments, then collected our gear and walked back to the beach house, where Leanna innocently asked how the snorkelling had gone. I explained, in a matter-of-fact way, that I'd nearly drowned, gave her the details without mentioning the "why not drown" voice, and emphasized that Jason had saved my life: never the wrong time for building family solidarities.

By the time we arrived at the wedding ceremony, everyone there seemed to know what had happened, even though I'd said nothing to anyone except Leanna. And since I was *at* the ceremony and not chilling in some hotel refrigerator, it seemed appropriate to deflect the "how do you feels?" and the implied "how could yous?" as politely as I could. I told people it had been foolish of me to go out that far, and left it at "I was an idiot." It was my son and new daughter-in-law's wedding, not my near-drowning and/or rescue that was being celebrated.

Maybe it was ducking that attention, and the reiterations—most of them my own—that I'd been a fool, that prevented me from burying what I'd done. The next morning, as I sat out on the beach house's yoga platform watching Jesse and his friends surf, the voice that had told me it would be okay to drown was still with me, the sensations interestingly raw and without conclusions. I had, for a few seconds—or was it several minutes—*wanted* to drown. Then some instincts, and some luck, interceded. What did it mean, and would it change me? What was I now supposed to do with this proof of human stupidity, fragility, and my own mortality? Get under the bed and stay there?

Nah. I haven't built a bulletproof closet so I can spend my days cowering, and I'm not wearing a life-saving vest on my evening walks. Almost drowning hasn't even kept me from snorkelling in Lake Erie—I do own that mask, after all, the damned thing cost a lot of money, and I am in that sense at least, my frugal father's son. I'm not about to go snorkelling again where only experienced surfers ought to be, but that's just my father and his ancestors kicking in again: common sense; don't knowingly put yourself in harm's way. I haven't taken any naps in pastures filled with wanting-to-rut bulls, nor do I cross busy streets walking backward with my eyes closed.

Still, by the time I stumbled out of the water that day and felt solid ground under my feet, I had a clearer understanding than at any point in my life that I have just this one to lose or give away or waste, and that I'm not any more immortal than my father turned out to be. This was something that his death had begun to bring home anyway; now it was beyond dispute. We can live our lives at an infinite range of velocities, and from nearly as many dispensations. But sooner or later, we all die.

That was the only conclusion possible to make, but it has brought neither comfort nor any sense of resolution with it. A day later, again sitting on the yoga platform, I came to another understanding, one that might be more important than the others: that context is everything, and maybe particularly when it concerns human happiness.

The difference between my kind of life and the kind of lives my parents had has everything to do with the context in which lives are lived and very little to do with knowledge or character. My father was a man who lived his life as if he were a riverboat captain, and never mind that his boat didn't have a motor. From where he started on the farm in northern Alberta he'd navigated his river to a sometimes unknowable but terminal *there*, and now, a *not-there*. But his life was what it became because he never let himself drift, never let up trying to steer his passage. He sought the river's strongest, surest currents with whatever resources he could deploy, and just as vigorously avoided whatever messes he detected. On balance, he was a good captain, and he was happy doing it because he believed he was always headed toward his goals. My mother did much the same with her life even though she didn't wave her captain's hat around the way my father did. She wanted to bear children, and she wanted to raise them on her terms. She got what she asked for, and she spent her life nurturing and protecting her children, more than occasionally against her selfish interest. When she wasn't making herself and everyone miserable with her refusal to bend to my father's will, she was happy living her life as she did, and she was good at it. Despite their war with one another, both of them were happy *in* the world as it presented itself. That their boat had no motor and was ultimately to go over the great Cosmic Waterfall is merely existential slapstick: the human condition.

I've lived my life in a world where no metaphors can convincingly energize individual purpose. In the place of purpose, there is an uneasily shared sense, particularly among the young, that the primary enterprise of the human species—our intelligence—may only be a short-term pollution of the planet, and on a trajectory no more noble than that of the dodo bird. There is no cosmic river for my kind to navigate, just like there is no cosmic surfing beach to drown myself on, and there are no gods worth beseeching or sassing. We're just messy-bags-of-mostly-carbon, trying to stay afloat in an ocean of undertows, crosstows, poisonous urchins, and mixed emotions. Or, put another way, there's just living and dying, memory and imagination, kindness and cruelty, and the requirement to plan one's passage through the mess of life even though there's no stable compass to do it with.

If I've learned anything from my parents' lives, and from their deaths, it is this: that everyone gets a unique hand to play, and the one I got isn't very much like the hands my parents were dealt, even though I'm an almost pure product of their being and their experience of the world. Unlike them, I can't take the world as it comes, because we've fouled it up so badly that we're constantly made aware of both its damaged condition and our complicity in making that way. We can't just take the world as it comes: we've got to try to repair it. But—and here's the news—we still have to make individual plans, and we still have to manipulate the things around us. We have to push and shove and do what we can, even though we're all eventually going headfirst into the big wall, slapstick style or over the Cosmic Waterfall. We still have to keep from tripping over our own feet while we try to figure out how we can go on living without it costing other people their health or their lives, and we have to find out if it's possible to repair the damage and clean up the mess we've made. But we may as well have a few laughs while we're doing that, and there's no point in taking ourselves very seriously.

So in that spirit, here's a laugh my father got from beyond the grave. When he retired in the late 1960s, he got himself the four things he'd wanted all his life: a Cadillac, an Airstream Trailer, a diamond ring, and a gold wristwatch. The Cadillacs and the Airstream you've heard about. The diamond ring, a big five-carat job, he wore every day until they took it away from him in the extended care facility. The wristwatch was a Rolex Oyster Perpetual Day-Date President with a 22-carat gold strap, about as ostentatious a watch as then existed. The strap, made of unusually soft, rich gold, had long ago fallen apart and been replaced by another, cheaper one. But he'd worn the watch until his eyes became so bad in his nineties he had to trade it in for a back-lit Timex with a face almost 3 inches across.

In his will, he bequeathed the diamond ring to my brother, and I got the Rolex and the carefully preserved gold strap, which had a note taped to it, written in his hand, explaining how valuable it was,

so don't throw it away. I accepted it graciously if not exactly gratefully, since the strap had broken down, the watch is far too grand
for my tastes, and in the circles I travel in, wearing a watch like it is
equivalent to putting a large sign on my back that reads "mug me."
Still, I understood what my duties were: I had to have the watch
evaluated for the estate, and there was a lesser duty to have the strap
repaired and the watch mechanism reconditioned so I could pass it
on to one of my sons in good working order at some future date so
he can be embarrassed by its grandness and not wear it either.

I took the watch to the Rolex store in Toronto after I got back
from Troncones to have both the evaluation and the reconditioning-
ing done at once. A nice young woman on the second floor took
the watch and told me to return in an hour for the evaluation and
the estimate for restoring it. Good service, I thought. A company
that takes its products seriously.

When I returned, I was confronted not by the young woman,
but by three men in suits, all with solemn expressions. "I'm afraid,"
the oldest of the three said, in an icy voice, "that we can't give you
an evaluation of this watch's value, and we can't repair it."

"Why's that?" I asked.

"Well," he said, staring at me as if I were some sort of master
criminal, "the serial numbers inside the casing of this watch have
been, ah, *defaced*."

I stared back at him for a moment, sifting through what I'd just
been told. "Let me get this straight," I said. "I just inherited the
watch from my father, who died a few months ago. He bought it in
Vancouver somewhere about 1967, and he wore it without incident
from that moment on. And you're telling me that he stole it?"

"We won't be able to trace the proper ownership," the man
said. "But yes, at some point this watch was stolen from its rightful
owner." His expression suggested that he thought I ought to crawl
under the table in shame because I wasn't its rightful owner, and

evidently had an intimate involvement with the criminal who'd been holding it for 40 years.

I began to laugh, helplessly and without a sliver of shame. My father had damned well known that his watch was hot. That was why he hadn't had the gold strap repaired. Chances are he'd never had the watch reconditioned, either, for the same reason. And he likely knew something like this was going to happen when I had it evaluated.

"My father was a Rotarian and a businessman," I told Rolex's three wise men, trying to keep a straight face. "I'm certain he didn't know it was stolen. It must have been a dishonest jeweller who tricked him into purchasing it. Unfortunately, I'm sure that jeweller is long gone, too, and impossible to trace."

The Rolex officials nodded, unforgivingly. I didn't believe a word of what I was saying, so I could hardly fault them if they didn't. My father wouldn't have given a damn about his watch being hot if it got him a hefty markdown on the price. And he would have found *this* moment particularly delicious, watching me lie through my teeth as I protested his honesty and respectability. I managed to get through a mostly straight-faced apology to the Rolex officials, took the watch back, and retreated. I hope they didn't hear me laughing as I went down the stairs, but I'd give anything if my father could have.

A Postscript

I'VE DELIBERATELY written this book with the flimsiest of outlines, and without any prearranged conclusions I was consciously or even unconsciously massaging the narrative to lead to. I didn't even hold a firm opinion about whether the lives of my two protagonists, Hartley Fawcett and Rita Surry, have anything profound to impart. So what did I find that is firm enough to put in a postscript as a conclusion?

Let me speak carefully: Hartley Fawcett and Rita Surry were *fulfilled* human beings who rarely worried about whether or not they were happy. They were engaged, busy, committed to near- and long-term goals that stayed pretty close to ground level. They were occasionally miserable, sure. But much more often they were cheerful and contented with their lot, sometimes unaccountably so in my mind. While they were alive, I had no idea how determined they'd been to do and get what they wanted, and how hard they'd worked at it. But for all that, they did *not* lead lives of epic proportion.

So let me argue their virtue in a slightly different context. We now live in a society—or rather, in loosely connected series of social, political, and cultural enclaves—atomized and reatomized by the unsleeping intrusions of mass media. Because we are so manipulated and our attentions so chronically interrupted, we are obsessed with making and maintaining connections; with social and economic networking; with accumulating and banking self-esteem, which we see as an acceptable substitute for human solidarities of different sorts. To this end we attempt to retribalize everything from the genome to our selection of tennis gear so we can get a leg-up on the next gang, and feel less lonely at the constant decay of our sense of connectedness with other people and things. We seek connections with our genetic ancestors, our ethnic forebears, we want intimacy with those who generations ago or last week were victimized along with us, and sometimes we seek amnesty from those we or our forebears have oppressed. Sometimes we and they, oppressed and oppressor, are one and the same.

Hartley Fawcett and Rita Surry experienced few of these things, but they had more singular ambitions for themselves than most people today. They undertook to build an entirely new world, and sometimes deliberately and sometimes indifferently, they turned their backs on everything that for us is regarded as the socially and psychologically acceptable means to achieve happiness.

That world they built, whether in the physical landscapes around me or inside my head—was stable and utterly safe. There was just the six of us, my parents, brother, my sisters, and me. In the summers, my maternal grandmother, Jessie, temporarily enlarged the family, and sometimes enriched it. The only other person I thought of as family was a man I knew only as "Uncle Willy," who wasn't a blood relative. He was a retired military officer who'd bonded with my parents while he was stationed in Prince George during the Second World War and afterward spent several weeks with us every second or third year until he died in the early 1960s.

There was a remarkable elasticity to this family that enabled it to weather the assaults of time and contingency. It could expand and contract without anxiety and without losing its integrity. Aunts, uncles, and cousins appeared from time to time, and were fed and bunked—then disappeared again without anyone quite thinking of them as family. Other people appeared and were accommodated, most of them young people—often immigrants—that my parents took under their wing. Some would become regulars for a year or two, others were more permanent. One family—the Tapps, an English mother and two sons who somehow landed up in the B.C. north after the war—had Christmas dinner with us for more than 20 years without anyone noticing the taps-and-faucets gag built into the family names. But really, it was the six of us that mattered, and I never looked beyond us, never felt the slightest sense of deprivation or isolation because I was not part of an extended family or ethnic group or even a religious denomination.

I think that the geographical—and cultural—isolation my parents deliberately chose was a powerful influence on their happiness, counterintuitive as that may seem. The distance they kept prevented the family demons from infecting their lives, and that of their children. It was their bulwark against the chaos of my mother's family and the entropy my father's family represented to him.

But there was more to it than intangibles. The distances kept away the mess, both in practical and psychological ways: the world where the generations before them and their own had butchered one another in wars and in ideological and racial pogroms and decades-long riots of authority. Because it was a frontier they lived on, hard work and enterprise could defend them against capricious men in corporate offices and stock markets. For a while, this was true.

My parents' plan was a risky one: all of it was up to Rita Surry and Hartley Fawcett, and it was *on* them if they failed.

These days, the nuclear family gets a lot of criticism for its tyrannies, which are much if not always well documented. But given their family pathologies, the nuclear family is what Hartley Fawcett and

Rita Surry chose to build with, and on balance, it worked. They tripped up on some day-to-daily stuff, and their one-to-one relationship was often miserable, but they made their family the core of their happiness, and it worked.

At the best of times, daily life tends to divorce people from the pursuit of happiness, and they weren't immune to that. But it's exactly here that the wilfulness of their overarching plan served them best. For most people of their generation, daily life was spent at wage labour tasks that held little interest beyond the paycheque, or in menial household stuff designed to keep boredom at bay. Those same things remain a factor today, although television and the half-assed interactivity of the Internet tend to keep us too addled with entertainment to notice that we've lost control of our lives in ways previous generations didn't have to worry about.

The kind of rights-based individuality that emerged after the Second World War is a factor, too. It has offered the individual vastly enhanced self-esteem, but it has tended to disable tangible connections with the world and with the participatory collectivities that can make daily life meaningful—the state, the city, the apparatuses that educate children, the neighbourhood, even the family. The largely heedless pursuit of self-esteem tends to bond us instead to abstractions like ethnicity, politicized religion, social democracy, capitalism, and a host of other partisanships which mostly find expression in excluding others from our gang. More than it ever was, daily life is the arena of the irritable, the disagreeable, and the venal: all the things there are no excuses for, and none of which contribute a thing to the pursuit of happiness, individual or collective.

That Hartley Fawcett and Rita Surry were happier than most of their generation is a subjective judgment for which I've provided, I hope, adequate evidence.

More important, I think, is that they grew old in a world that had begun with them, and they died believing that there was a decent probability that what they had built would continue beyond them: so far, so good. At the very least, the baseless, groundless happiness I experience at being in the world is a proof that the world they created does travel on, immune to the miseries of daily life and the mess we've made of things. Of all the gifts they conferred on me, this barely tangible one often seems the most valuable. I have no guarantee that things will be alright, but it is built into my character that life is worth working at, even when it contradicts most of what I've learned.

Here in the twenty-first century, airborne acids eat the headstones and the monuments of what and who is dead and past, slowly erasing the carved names, including, eventually, those of my parents. That's mortality: the way things are.

My mother, uninterested in monuments, wanted her ashes scattered over the hillside where she'd picked wild asparagus; no stone, no wasted plot of ground for her. If anyone wants to visit her now, they'll have to go out in the world, to exactly the spot—and the kind of spot—where she liked the world best. My father, always lonely for company (or an audience to whom he could sell something), asked for a niche and a plaque in a mausoleum, albeit one with a view for the days when no one comes to visit and he's bored with the silence of his neighbours. Few will visit his out-of-the-way spot, but no matter. He'll live on inside the heads of everyone in his family for generations to come, even when they've ceased to know his name. I watched my daughter playing cards at the dining room table recently, and saw his hand move hers, and caught his sly grin on her face. Earlier that same evening, I'd found her humming as she dried the dinner dishes, and it was my mother's voice I heard.

I think that's all we get—that and the epic labour of living, and the laughter, and the mess. It's enough.

The Closet

BOTH SIDES of my father's family have deep and typical roots in Canada. One side came from Ireland between 1845 and 1847, driven to emigrate by the Potato Famine. The other side came from Scotland's Western Islands, victims of the Clearances at the end of the eighteenth century. Both ended up farming near Georgian Bay on Ontario's Lake Huron.

My grandfather, Tom Fawcett, had a rough childhood after his father died in an 1862 farming accident when Tom was two—and after his mother, within a year, married a widower with ten children of his own. But he survived, and in 1894 got lucky for the first—and maybe only—time in his life, when he courted and married Leila McPhadon. In marrying Tom Fawcett, Leila was marrying down, and her family probably wasn't happy about the union. But with the deed done, the pragmatic McPhadons accepted Tom. When Leila's father, Duncan, decided to move his part of the clan to Alberta in 1899, Tom and Leila went with them. My father, the youngest of six children, was born in Edmonton in the spring of 1907. The extended family lived in Edmonton until one after another, they began buying and clearing quarter sections of farmland 40 kilometres north of the city, between the

French-speaking enclaves of Morinville and Riviere Qui Barre.

Life wasn't sweet on newly cleared grain farms in northern Alberta at the turn of the twentieth century. There was little money and endless labour and my father and his three older brothers were expected to do much of the latter for none of the former. When he was 14, my father asked tight-fisted Tom for money so he could get a haircut and go to the Sunday baseball game. Tom said no, and when my father challenged him, a brawl ensued. It ended with my father getting his face pushed into the mud at the end of the wooden sidewalk that ran from the house halfway to the barn. He got to his feet, shook his fist at his father, and walked away. He never, by his account, lived under his father's roof again.

The truth is more complicated. My father was a mama's boy, and he did return home, then and in the next decades, to see Leila—just as, the story goes, he'd returned home from his first year of elementary school at lunch hour to breastfeed. Mostly he visited while his father was out in the fields, but he also came home for family events, always, he said, keeping a physical distance between himself and his father.

He worked on neighbours' farms around Riviere Qui Barre until he moved into Edmonton, took a short course in heavy mechanics, and before he was out of his teens he was making a living fixing cars in the back alleys. He began to buy and sell cars and motorcycles, bought an Indian motorcycle for himself and rode it all over northern Alberta on the territory's dual-rut muddy frontier roads.

My father's brothers were soft-spoken Presbyterian pragmatists who married big-bodied women from the French-Canadian community that had settled St. Albert and Morinville decades before. The brothers orbited their women, playing baseball in the summer and endless card games through the longer winters, dutifully coming home whenever Leila summoned them. Elmer, my father's oldest sibling, was the gentlest of the brothers, and the only one with whom I spent any time. He was a serious ballplayer and until he lost his right index finger in a coal-mining mishap, the best pitcher in northern Alberta.

"I didn't have much of a curveball after I lost that finger," he told me ruefully when he was 89 and in a rest home. It was one of the few memories—or regrets—he seemed to have, and the only story he ever told me. Elmer is on the far left of the photo. My father is on the far right.

I never heard about the biggest adventure of his life until after he was dead. In the spring of 1918, he and younger brother Alex disappeared into the bush near Hinton to avoid being drafted into the army and sent to France. I don't know what Alex's motives were, but I'm pretty sure Elmer took off because he didn't want to hurt anyone. The brothers didn't come out until the fall of 1919, but all they offered my father about their adventure were laconic complaints about not getting enough to eat. They had nothing to say about how good the deer they shot tasted, or how stringy the moose meat was. They just weren't storytellers.

The only other family stories come from the McPhadon side, like the one about Uncle Dan, Leila's older brother, who wandered into the jungles of Madagascar in 1896 and was murdered. No one seemed to know why, or who killed him. Natives? Other adventurers? No one was even a little curious: Uncle Dan was in some dangerous foreign land, and something bad happened. What was he thinking, taking chances like that? These were

people who lived with stolid, decent Presbyterian values: Don't
expect much from God, work hard when you must, get ahead
if you can, don't put yourself in harm's way, die when your time
comes.

*   *   *

My mother's background is also typical of Canada, but the central characters were anything but stolid and Presbyterian. She
was born Rita Joan Surry on April 19, 1910, in Seattle, Washing-
ton, of English parents on their way to settle, in a roundabout
way, in eastern Alberta. She grew up in a series of rural Alberta
towns where her father taught school and her mother—who was
her father's second wife and 18 years his junior, gave music lessons
and tried to keep order in a growing household without much
money. Rita was the fourth of eight children. Her two half-
brothers, Norman and Douglas, her father's sons by his first marriage, were gone before she was five years old. Douglas died of a
bowel obstruction at age 19 in 1915, while Norman, who enlisted
to fight in the Great War in 1914, was killed in combat in France
in 1918, a few weeks before it ended. He was 24 years old. Rita
grew up as the den mother to her older and slightly delicate
brother, Alan, younger sisters Enid and Daphne, and younger
brothers Ronald and Hector.

All of this is fact, and on the surface, common enough for those
who chose to emigrate from Edwardian England. But there is star-
tlingly little of it that remains stable under scrutiny, and there are
two versions of the family history. One is the Official History, the
other is the one no one talked about even if they knew what was
in it. The Official History smoothed the facts to suit the identities of my mother's parents, Frederic Robert Surry and Jessie
Florence Loe, wanted to project—and to hide the skeletons rat-

tling noisily in the closet. Fred and Jessie presented themselves as exiled scions of the English upper classes, people so well educated and cultured that it's hard to believe they could have left England at all, and harder still to imagine how they survived the barbarous wilderness they found themselves in. In their minds, they were emigrants *from* England, not immigrants *to* Canada. They remained determinedly English all their lives, ex-patriot pillars of Edwardian moral values.

They were anything but. Fred (who expected to be called Mr. Surry, and was therefore called "Fred" by all his Canadian neighbours) and Jessie Surry were complex and irascible people. And they were liars.

How Fred and Jessie found each other is pure fairy tale. Shortly after the turn of the century, Jessie Loe had been taken on as a student teacher in music in the London public school at which Oxford-educated Fred was headmaster. The two became friends, mostly through a common love of music—Fred played the violin, Jesse piano. During those years, Fred's first wife had a nervous breakdown, was institutionalized in an asylum, and died shortly thereafter. Around the same time, Jessie contracted tuberculosis, and spent two years recuperating in a sanitarium. While she was there, Fred visited, and a platonic relationship that included reading Shakespeare's plays and sonnets together gradually blossomed into romantic love. When Jessie's lungs healed, she and the now-widower Fred married; after an appropriate interval. After another appropriate interval, their first child together was born. It was then that they decided to emigrate to a dryer climate to protect Jessie's frail lungs. They chose Alberta over Australia, partly because Canada was closer to England, and partly because of the presence of Fred's brother Vincent in Seattle, which the newlyweds, used to English distances, mistook for a short jaunt from Alberta.

For 13 years, Fred Surry taught in one remote Alberta town after another. Wherever they were, he and Jessie did what they could to enrich the lives of their students and the larger community by teaching a much wider range of subjects than the Alberta curriculum required, and by organizing musical afternoons and soirees. Jessie also did her best to feed whatever poor children came around, and they added to their own growing brood. Enid was born in 1914, and the birth of two sons, Hector and Ronald, followed in 1917 and 1918. Alas (a word often heard in Official Histories), the strain of bearing Ronald undermined Jessie's health, and custody of Hector was temporarily surrendered to a childless neighbour, who promptly pulled up stakes and moved to the United States, taking Hector with them.

There was other trouble. Their marriage was soured by Fred's grief at the loss of the two sons by his first wife, and by his coldness and indifference toward his second family after the second son Norman's death in 1918. Any extra money the pair earned after that was sent to the British widow and child Norman left behind. Fred, meanwhile, was particularly vicious toward Alan, his first-born son by Jessie, and he is said to have tacitly encouraged the abduction of Hector. Jessie seems never to have forgiven him for the loss of Hector or for his mistreatment of Alan, and later on, for disinheriting my mother. She was said to be more bitter still about having to support her stepson's widow while they lived in such depressing conditions themselves.

Most of this is heavily laced with malarkey. First of all, Fred's first marriage didn't end because his wife died, but because she had a drinking problem, for which vice British women were then placed in insane asylums as "dipsomaniacs." Fred may have had Alice committed, but Alice didn't, as in the Official History, die "shortly after." She recovered, was released from the asylum—

if she was ever in one—and lived until April 1922, in Chiswick, Middlesex, where, according to her death certificate, she'd been running a boarding house. Chiswick is the downtown London neighbourhood where E.M. Forster grew up, and where Alexander Pope once resided.

Jessie Loe did spend some time in a tubercular sanitarium, but it wasn't quite concern for her health that precipitated emigration. She'd become pregnant in the late summer of 1908 while Fred was teaching in an obscure school at Bexhill, near Hastings in Sussex. He was terminated from this post for his "indifferent teaching habits"—likely code for the fact that he was living out of wedlock with a pregnant woman 18 years his junior.

Jessie was already pregnant with my mother when they docked at Quebec City—she might have been conceived in the middle of the Atlantic—and the trip to Seattle the following spring was probably made as much to allow Jessie to give birth under more civilized conditions as to renew contact with Fred's younger brother, Vincent, who, in the real world, had left England around 1890 under a cloud of his own. Among other misbehaviours, he'd been drummed out of teaching for the same sort of indifference that marked Fred's early teaching career, and is reputed to have spent his honeymoon whoring in the cathouses of Paris.

Fred Surry, you may have noticed, wasn't quite a nobly educated public school headmaster either. He'd attended Culham College, a teacher-training institute distantly attached to Oxford, and the college records mark him as "indolent and unpunctual." There is no evidence to suggest that he'd ever taught at a prominent public school, and some 2+2=4 reasonings suggest that it was Jessie's pregnancy and the crisis that precipitated that made them emigrate to Canada. In Edwardian England, it was quite a lot more than "socially unconventional" for a couple to live out of wedlock. It was unlawful, and Fred and Jessie must have realized that they would have no kind of life in England with that hanging over their heads.

But from here, the facts begin to sweeten. Pre-emigration Fred Surry might have been a philanderer and a rounder, but the circumstances he found himself in made him a different man. He became an omnivorous reader, and he mastered and then taught a broad range of subject matter over the years, from English literature and philology, through astronomy, math, and physics. There are numerous testimonials from rural Alberta's extensive local history documents that he taught them well. He transformed himself from the flaky ne'er-do-well he arrived as into a real and convincing paragon of British Imperial culture and formality over the last 35 years of his life. He got, as they say, serious.

In the real world, Fred Surry and Jessie Loe were both products of England's lower middle class. Jessie's family had been milliners and sometimes printers in downtown London, and Fred, though the family legend has him as one of a long line of educators, turns out to be the descendant of Suffolk coastguardsmen, men who, since the fifteenth century, rescued foundering mariners with small boats, often perishing themselves in the attempt. One of them married a teacher in the eighteenth century, thus adding a little culture to the operant family character, which was most firmly marked, into my mother's generation, by that mariners' cold courage in the face of mortal danger.

Fred and Jessie weren't legally married, and the children of their union were therefore illegitimate. But a year or so after they were notified of the death of Fred's first wife, they held a formal wedding ceremony in Edmonton's grandest Anglican church, and a few weeks later, had the children baptized in the same church. Much later, my mother passed the marriage off as a "renewal of vows," and explained away the baptisms by saying, well, living in the country gave them no time for frills like that, eh? In 1927, the newlyweds returned to England for a two-month visit, where it is clear that both families welcomed them with great affection. The English are strange people.

In the only photograph that has survived of Jessie Loe and Fred Surry together, they seem physically mismatched. Jessie, who was five feet ten inches tall, gazes frankly at the camera with a slight but interested smile on her face. Her hair is dark, and she is wearing a light-coloured sweater and skirt, very plain, that does not hide her big-boned frame, nor the distinct directness of her bearing. Fred is several inches shorter, and leans away from the camera. He is slight, white-haired, a white handlebar moustache hiding his pursed lips. His brow is furrowed, his hands are thrust deep enough into the pockets of his baggy three-button suit jacket for him to be fiddling with the family jewels, and he seems to be wondering if the person taking the picture is competent. The only way I can date the photo in the mid-1920s is that between them, standing on a chair and smiling uncertainly, is skinny four- or five-year-old Daphne, their youngest daughter.

When I first met Daphne, in 1959, she struck me as both attractive and unsettling—she had an unpredictable and acerbic wit that was mischievously funny and unpleasant moment by moment. She'd been a successful CBC radio host in Alberta during the 1950s, and was headed for the big time as a national morning-show host when her marriage fell apart. The insult of that destroyed her confidence and unleashed a stream of misanthropic acid that, literally, poisoned her career and the rest of her private life. When I saw her next, during a 1998 visit along with my mother, she weighed nearly 300 pounds, her health was failing, and she spoke disparagingly about everyone my mother mentioned, including her own children and grandchildren. Through most of the visit, she kept glancing at the television, and I could see she wanted to get back to the cartoons she'd been watching on video when we arrived.

I record this not to single her out as a Jenny Craig or Dr. Phil rehab target, but because she was characteristic of the Surrys. They were talented and intelligent and extremely verbal. They could withstand physical blows, and all of them were as unafraid of dying as their coastguardsmen ancestors. But they were emotionally fragile. Save for the two half-brothers, who died too young for anyone to know what they'd have done with their lives, all of them died from emotional blows—and from whatever it was in them that, after mortal insults or emotional trauma, left them unable to cope with daily life.

Fred Surry's body may have been interred in 1944, but my mother insisted that the essential part of him died in 1918 when he received the news that his favourite son had been killed in France. There were other dark currents within him—among them a pathological jealousy that made him doubt the paternity of his own children, perhaps to the point of giving one of them, Hector, away. As an adult, Hector looked least like the Surrys, and the one or two photos that have survived of him as an infant are similarly distinctive. And really, with an irascible, jealous husband nearly two decades her senior, who can say what went on in Jessie's mind and heart, or what she might have done to spite him?

Fred's other two late-born sons spent the Second World War trying to get themselves killed. The eldest, Alan, was a sergeant in the artillery, and during a battle in Italy had every stitch of clothing, save one of his boots, blown off when an enemy shell landed near his gun. The concussion from the shell killed everyone else in his gun crew, and Alan himself sustained both serious burns and some permanent hearing loss. He returned to combat sooner than he needed to, without a qualm. What did break him was that during his convalescence in England, he met and fell in love with the daughter of Jessie's sister—a first cousin named Jessie Palmer. They decided that they couldn't marry because of the kinship proximity, and Alan returned to Canada after the war, permanently pissed off at the world. He married and had a family anyway, but soon began drinking heavily, and was dead by 1958. Jessie Palmer, a beautiful, delicate woman, never married either. When my father met her in 1960, he clumsily asked her why she hadn't.

"I couldn't have the man I preferred," she answered.

Ronald, the youngest son, survived until 1989, but left a similar trail of mayhem in his wake, abandoning a wife and two small sons in Canada for a British war widow so beautiful she took my breath away when I first met her in 1962. He ruined this second marriage and alienated their daughter with jealousy and the acid outbursts of temper that he seemed, like all the Surrys, disinclined to control.

The second of the three sisters, Enid, was the prettiest of the daughters, and by most accounts, the one with the greatest intelligence, the most vitality—and the foulest mouth. She married at 19, had five daughters in seven years, and when her husband marched off to war—a little too cheerfully to suit her—she spent the balance of the war getting revenge for his unfaithfulness by indulging her appetites. She gained 100 pounds over the next decade, and even though she remarried and had a son in 1952 with a second husband who adored her, she never quite forgave the world for its insults. The only time my mother left me alone with Enid was when I was 12. She spent the whole time telling me dirty jokes I was too young to understand, although I do remember her merry hoots of laughter as she rattled them off.

All of the Surrys—from Fred and Jessie down through their children, were high-strung and permanently restless; all of them were prone to take offence and more prone to hold grudges. All had acid tongues that made them entertaining and funny one moment, viciously cruel the next. Jessie and Fred had the ugly habit of playing their children off against one another, picking favourites and cruelly flaunting it to the unfavoured ones. Early on, Fred and Jessie had tagged my mother as the "family drone," the untalented dummy. She struggled at school, and possessed none of the artistic facility the others showed. "My parents always looked at me and said, 'How could we have had a child like you?'" She once said to me, "But you see, intelligence and talent aren't necessarily strong, and they aren't necessarily wise."

*   *   *

In October 2009, I visited the graves of three of my grandparents in Edmonton. I was taken to them by Brian Manson, the cousin who has made himself the keeper of our family's forgotten or unlamented dead—which, by now, you know are legion. At the time, Brian was himself going through a messy end to his 40-year marriage. I'd flown out to help him get through it, and both of us were in need of distraction, even if it was going to be the morbid kind. The weather that day was suitably overcast and chilly, leaves blowing on the wind, and neither of our spirits much more anchored. I'd never been to any of the graves before.

The first two were in Mount Pleasant cemetery, on Edmonton's south side, the graves of my paternal grandparents, Thomas Robert Fawcett and Leila McPhadon. They died within a few months of one another in 1948, Leila first, then Tom. "He gave up because he was too damned lazy to go on without her," my father once said of him. It was probably sweeter than that, but since he knew his father, and I never met him, I didn't argue.

Tom and Leila had company, although none of their children—likewise all dead now—are buried there. Leila's father and mother, Duncan McPhadon and Janet Davidson, the family patriarch and matriarch, are 2 metres away, beneath a larger headstone of the same black marble. Hester Weir, Leila's younger sister and the only member of her generation I ever saw in the flesh, is also a few plots away, along with a half-dozen others from the family she married into.

I felt a twinge as I leaned over to touch Hester's headstone. I'd tagged along with her on a trip to an Edmonton corner store in the late 1950s, when she was in her mid-eighties. She was a tiny woman who walked so quickly I had trouble keeping up, and she talked a blue streak the whole time. She was fond of Jean Beliveau, the Montreal Canadiens' captain, knew all his scoring statistics, and gave me a credible demonstration of the way he stickhandled with the puck unusually far in front of him. She'd had a tough life, Hester, losing her husband when she was in her early thirties. She raised their son without complaining and apparently without ever considering remarriage. She lasted until she was 93, by at least one account with her faculties merrily intact, including the crush on Jean Beliveau.

I was four years old when Leila McPhadon and Tom Fawcett died, and this was the closest I'd ever been to them. My father went back for his mother's funeral alone, and he didn't return for his father's funeral a few months later. I asked him, in the year before he died, what the last thing he ever said to his father had been.

"The same thing I said when I left home," he answered. "Go to hell."

Knowing him, he probably said it across his mother's casket. The two of them had been at it for a quarter century by then, but it wasn't the longest fight of my father's career. The one with me was closing in on 50 years before it petered out, and the war with my mother had gone on longer than that. All were struggles for or against independence, but only that first one was decisive.

The third grave was across town, in the grander Edmonton municipal cemetery, not far from several hundred military graves, most of them veterans of the First World War who hadn't survived it long—their lungs fouled by poison gas or their minds and bodies broken by combat. Brian and I wandered among the military graves for a few minutes trying to imagine the pain-filled lives of which the laconic inscriptions on the headstones revealed so little, and then he walked me to the grave of our common maternal grandfather, Fred Surry, who died a few months before I was born in 1944. Fred's remains had been there for more than a half century before Brian buried his mother's ashes in the same plot in 1999—fitting, since she'd been his favoured daughter.

All four of my grandparents had relatively long lives, and ones that had their share of bitterness and regret. Jessie, my mother's mother, lasted the longest—she was 99 when she died in 1983. I know something of the hardships they endured, but almost nothing about what pleased them, and nothing at all about their terrors or their raptures. I assume they had their raptures, because no one lives as long as they did without them. But it is their terrors and their regrets that are easier to imagine. Did Tom Fawcett awaken in the night, assaulted by nightmares created in shadows in the stables he'd slept in, neglected and unloved, as a child? Did Leila dream of luxuriating in her father Duncan's lap in the hours before her death? How many times had Fred Surry awakened at night, his heart pounding as he witnessed machine-gun bullets ripping apart his beloved son as he tried to lead his men across that French roadway in 1918? Was there an afternoon similar to this one, say, when Leila stared at Duncan's grave with the same emotions that I feel now? Or did she merely wonder if she'd done or said enough to him while he was alive to make him feel adequately cared for as his life slipped away? And what was it that these people thought about as they felt their own lives ebbing, slipping inexorably toward the darkness that is the only thing, in the end, we are sure to share? Was Fred Surry, in the infinitely elastic second when the broken muscles of his heart flooded the aortic chambers with the plasmic chaos that ended his life, filled with longing for his favourite son, or did he regret his destructive jealousy, his mistreatment of his second family, or plead for forgiveness to the daughter he'd disinherited or the sons he'd given or driven away?

What I *can* understand is how deep and profound the continuum is that I share with those ancestors, and how it is at once utterly particular and interconnected. Hartley Fawcett and Rita Surry were the products of those lived lives, in exactly the same way that I'm the product of theirs. And here I have a useful insight: Leila, Tom, Fred, and Jesse experienced some degree of delight and even rapture—on the evidence that I've been able to unearth, Leila and Jesse more than their men, one of whom, Tom, was too damaged to experience much of anything, while Fred was too crazy; the women were simply better equipped and less damaged than their men. Fuelled with this and by what were probably the most basic of nurturing instincts, they operated domestic matriarchies inside the brutish patriarchies that surrounded and ruled them all. Jessie's example encouraged my mother to create something similar, and Leila's example convinced my father, the strongest personality of any of them, not to interfere while he built his business empire around it. My parents, determined not to live with the miseries their parents did, formed a partnership and made a conscious plan for their lives together.

ENDNOTE

This has been the loneliest book I've ever written. It was composed in a no-man's-land boundaried by privacy (mine and other people's); the danger of indiscreet disclosure; what I used to think of as "literature"; and the not entirely genial pressure of the marketplace, which assumes that readers have become as dumb as shoppers, and therefore demand thematic simplicity no matter what has to be sacrificed to get it.

I have had readers: Stan Persky, who reads everything I write; Karen Mulhallen, who has seen versions of different elements of the book over a 20-year period; and my wife, Leanna Crouch. Each of them, by telling me I had a necessary story to tell, have forced me to make sense of it. I'm also grateful to my cousin Brian Manson, who almost single-handedly unlocked the family closet, and when I opened it, helped me to identify the skeletons as they tumbled out.

I'd thank the central characters in this narrative, my parents, Hartley Fawcett and Rita Surry, but they're not listening. I continue to love them and miss their counsel despite their incomprehensible silence. Neither of them took mortal offence at my shenanigans while they were alive, and would most likely enjoy the exercise they've gotten in these pages. If I've offended any living members of my extended family, I apologize, but must ultimately excuse myself in the name of art, love, and hopefully, truth.

I'd also like to thank the nameless gods of comedy, who, inconstant as they are, have presided over most of this. For all their caprice and cruelty, they're the only abstractions worthy of our admiration and loyalty.

I didn't begin this book with firm beliefs about human happiness, and I remain agnostic. I've pretty much lived my life without the dubious benefits of ideology, and I've never harboured the hope that there might be divine design at work or even play. I simply don't have illusions about how life is *supposed* to go. We are what we do, we get what we make of things: *we mostly run, we mostly fall,* hopefully down some stairs in a public place so others can enjoy a few laughs.

I do believe that kindness and laughter make the arbitrariness of life easier to survive, but I have only anecdotal evidence for this. Hence this has been a navigation without a map, utterly unguided by a philosophy or a 12-step program. Where this book has been governed by principle, it is the one I gleaned from what my parents taught me about the world: that one can help oneself and others, but then a bus can run us down or those we love. Cool dry days are better for love and war alike. Rainy days serve best for thinking, but only if and when there's will. To ask for more would betray what they gave me.